Student Workbook

Strengthening Family & Self

Teacher's Annotated Workbook

Sixth Edition

LEONA JOHNSON, EdS
Beldenville, Wisconsin

Publisher
The Goodheart-Willcox Company, Inc.
Tinley Park, Illinois
www.g-w.com

Introduction

This *Student Workbook* is designed for use with the text *Strengthening Family & Self*. It will help you recall and review concepts presented in the text. It will also help you apply what you learn to real-life situations.

This *Workbook* is divided into chapters that correspond to the chapters in the text. Each chapter contains one or more activities for each section in the chapter. By reading the text first, you will have the information you need to complete the activities. Try to complete the activities without referring to the text. If necessary, you can look at the text again later to complete any activities you could not finish.

Some of the activities in this *Workbook*, such as matching and crossword puzzles, require factual answers. You can use these activities as review guides for tests and quizzes. Other activities ask for opinions, evaluations, and conclusions. These activities have neither right nor wrong answers since they are designed to stimulate your thinking and help you apply information presented in the text.

The challenging activities in this *Workbook* will allow you to express your creativity and develop skills for daily living. The more thought you put into these activities, the more you will learn from them.

Contents

Chapter 1

A Close-Up View of You

Your Life Path

Activity A

Section 1:1

Name _____

Date _____ Period _____

Diagram your own life path, starting with birth and ending with death. Above the line, write major events that you remember from your past near the appropriate age. Also add major events that you would like to see or expect to occur in your future. Put an approximate age or date at which you would like to see these events take place. Below the line, list people who were or will be affected by your actions at each state. Then describe what the family can do to promote growth and development at that stage.

(Student response.)

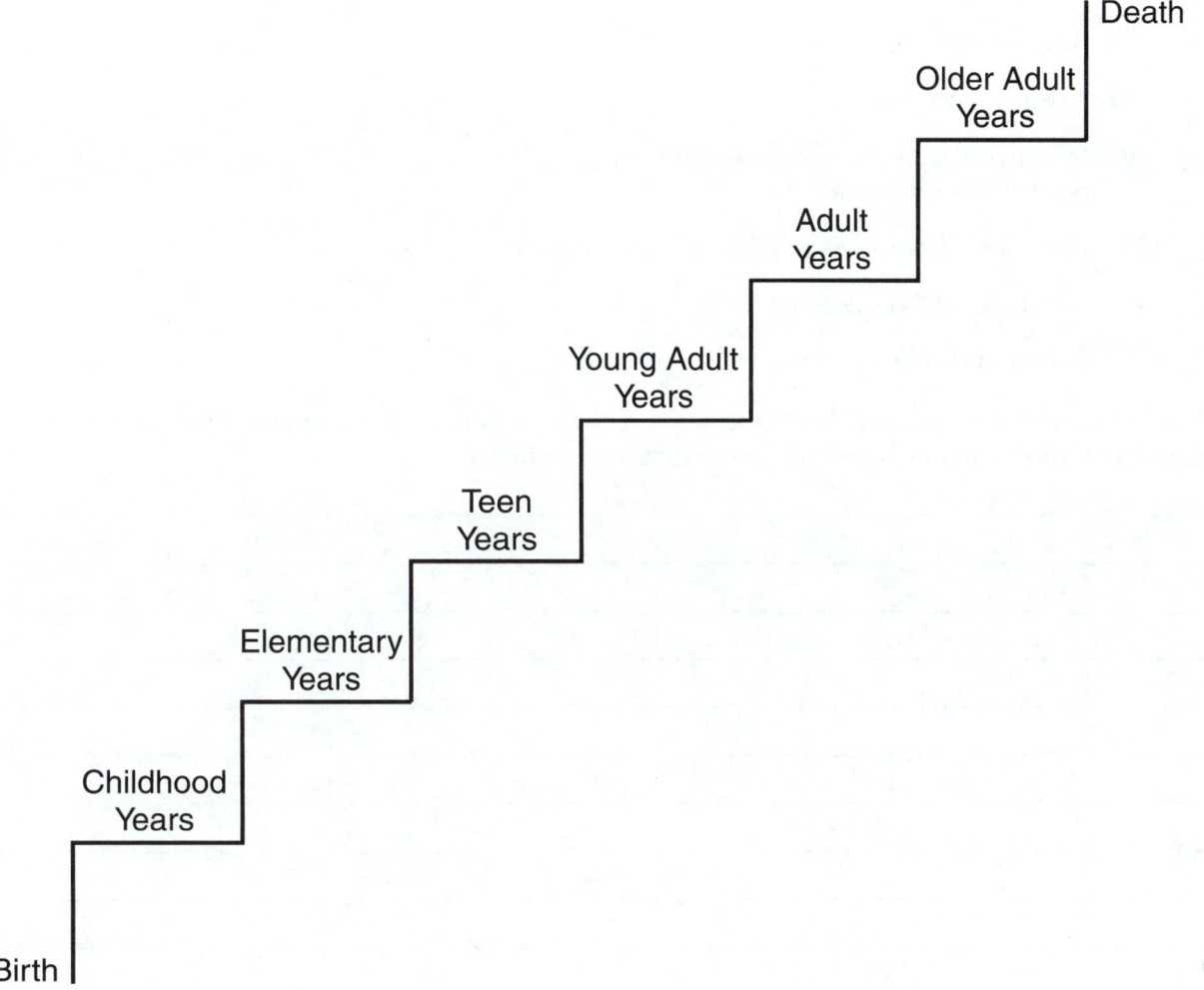

Understanding the Developmental Tasks of Teens

Activity B

Name _____

Section 1:1

Date _____ **Period** _____

Read each problem described below. Identify the developmental task that relates to that problem area and place the appropriate letter in the blank. The developmental tasks can be used more than once.

Developmental Tasks of Teens

A. understand and accept who you are

B. make healthful choices that help you grow to maturity

C. develop mature relationships with others

D. prepare for an occupation

E. prepare for marriage and family living

___B___ 1. Chooses a candy bar and soda for breakfast.

___A___ 2. Has low self-esteem.

___E___ 3. Learns that he or she will have a child.

___B___ 4. Uses tobacco.

___C___ 5. Fights with peers.

___D___ 6. Does not study or perform well in school.

___B___ 7. Abuses alcohol.

___C___ 8. Argues with parents.

___A___ 9. Is self-centered and conceited, and recognizes no faults.

___C___ 10. Does not believe anyone will love him or her.

___B___ 11. Eats little and diets constantly.

___D___ 12. Does not develop excellence in any skill.

13. Choose one of the above problems and write a paragraph describing how the problem could interfere with the achievement of the developmental tasks.

(Student response.) _____

_____

_____

_____

_____

_____

_____

_____

_____

Managing the Process of Change

Activity C

Section 1:1

Name _____

Date _____ Period _____

Life is full of transitions—changes from one situation to another. How will you manage these changes? Planning and preparing ahead may help you manage feelings of fear or discomfort that often come with making changes. Think of a change you expect to happen in the near future. (For example, moving to a new school, a change in a relationship, a change in a role, or a new routine.) Answer the following questions honestly to help you manage the transition.

The Situation

1. Identify the next big change or transition you expect to go through in the future. (Student response.)

   _____

   _____

   _____

2. In what ways will your routines change when this transition takes place? (Student response.)

   _____

   _____

   _____

3. How will your roles as an individual, family member, friend, and any other roles you fill change with this transition? (Student response.)

   _____

   _____

4. In what ways will your relationships change? (Student response.)

   _____

   _____

   _____

5. What other events could add stress to your life while this transition is taking place? (Student response.)

   _____

   _____

   _____

Personal Feelings

6. How do big changes usually make you feel? (Student response.)

   _____

   _____

   _____

(Continued)

7. Would you describe your feelings as generally positive or negative when big changes take place? (Student response.)

_____

_____

Help from Others

8. Who are the people you can talk to (family, relatives, friends) when going through a big change?

9. Will there be any changes in the support these people give after the transition takes place? (Student response.)

_____

_____

10. What steps could you take to build a stronger support group to help you through a big change or transition in life? (Student response.)

_____

_____

_____

A Plan of Action

11. List the information you would need to know about this future change to help you make the transition smoothly. (Student response.)

_____

_____

_____

12. Identify one or more sources where this information could be obtained. (Student response.)

_____

_____

_____

13. What skills or qualities could help you make this change smoothly? (Student response.)

_____

_____

_____

_____

Heredity

Activity D

Section 1:2

Name_____

Date _____ Period _____

Identify the following traits as being dominant or recessive. Place *D* in the blank if the trait is dominant or *R* if the trait is recessive.

_**D**_ 1. Farsightedness

_**D**_ 2. Black hair

_**D**_ 3. Freckles

_**R**_ 4. Short thin eyelashes

_**R**_ 5. Broad nose

_**R**_ 6. Flat feet

_**R**_ 7. Blue eyes

_**D**_ 8. Dimples in cheeks

_**R**_ 9. Normal vision

_**D**_ 10. Curly hair

Use the Punnett square to complete the following activity. Identify the changes a color-blind male (cXY) and a carrier female (CcXX) have for producing color-blind children. The female's father is color-blind, but she is not.

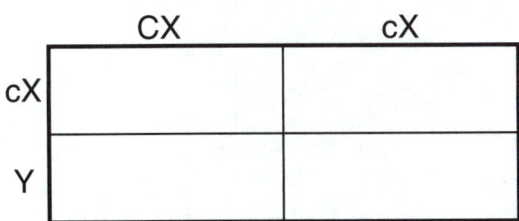

XX = female

XY = male

CC = normal

Cc = carrier with normal vision

cc = color-blind

Results: Number of chances out of 4

Percent Chance

11. ___**1**___ /4 will be females with normal vision

12. ___**1**___ /4 will be carrier females

13. ___**1**___ /4 will be color-blind females

14. ___**1**___ /4 will be males with normal vision

15. ___**1**___ /4 will be color-blind males

16. ___**0**___ /4 will be carrier males

___**25%**___

___**25%**___

___**25%**___

___**25%**___

___**25%**___

___**0%**___

17. What is the advantage of knowing the chances for having a child with a hereditary disease?
might impact whether you have children

18. Why do you think an insurance company would want to know your chances of having a child with a hereditary disease? **Insurance companies want to know if risk of disease might increase their costs.**

19. In what ways might genetic technologies interfere with a person's right to privacy? **The presence of certain genes might indicate possible diseases that might prevent a person from getting insurance.**

A Close-Up View of You

Activity E Name ____________________

Section 1:3 Date ______________ Period ______________

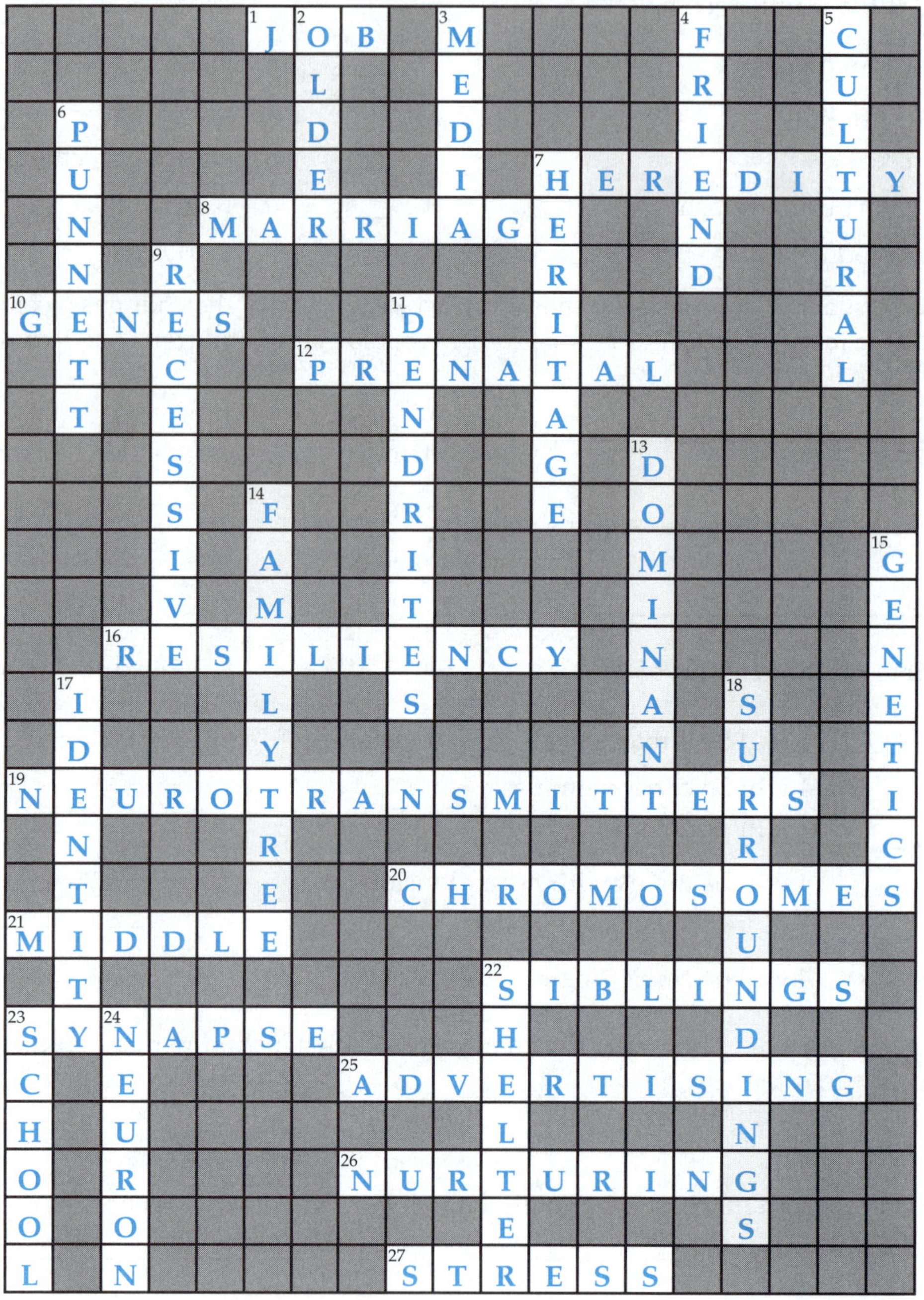
1 JOB
2 OLDER
3 MEDIA
4 FRIEND
5 CULTURAL
6 PUNNETT
7 HEREDITY
7 HERITAGE
8 MARRIAGE
9 RECESSIVE
10 GENES
11 DENDRITES
12 PRENATAL
13 DOMINANT
14 FAMILY TREE
15 GENETICS
16 RESILIENCY
17 IDENTITY
18 SURROUNDINGS
19 NEUROTRANSMITTERS
20 CHROMOSOMES
21 MIDDLE
22 SIBLINGS
22 SHELTER
23 SYNAPSE
23 SCHOOL
24 NEURON
25 ADVERTISING
26 NURTURING
27 STRESS

(Continued)

Read the descriptions and decide which chapter terms are being described. Write the correct terms in the crossword puzzle.

Across

1. A person's _____ is an important environmental influence during the adult years.

7. The sum of the qualities that have been passed on from your ancestors through your parents to you.

8. Close relationships help prepare young adults for _____.

10. _____ are the basic units of heredity.

12. A healthful _____ environment is important to a child before birth.

16. The ability to adjust to setbacks and make changes to reach maximum growth and development is called _____.

19. _____ are chemicals that carry information between nerve cells.

20. A person inherits 23 _____ from each parent.

21. _____ children often find themselves being peacemakers.

22. _____ are brothers and sisters.

23. The space between two neurons is called a _____.

25. _____ can influence a person's buying decisions.

26. A family environment needs to be loving and _____.

27. Extreme or long-term _____ can have a negative effect on a child's development.

Down

2. _____ siblings may be given more responsibility.

3. _____ resources include television, newspapers, radio, and the Internet.

4. Peers can help you know what qualities you like in a _____.

5. Your family's guidelines and beliefs are part of your _____ heritage.

6. A _____ square is used to determine gene combinations.

7. Your cultural _____ is learned behavior that is passed on from generation to generation.

9. _____ genes determine the nature of a trait only when two of them are present.

11. _____ are parts of a neuron that receive information from another nerve cell.

13. Genes that are _____ determine the nature of a trait.

14. Your _____ _____ is a list of your blood relatives.

15. _____ is the study of how genes are passed on through the generations.

17. A sense of individuality is called self-_____.

18. Your environment includes your _____ and everything in them.

22. A family should meet needs for food, clothing, and _____.

23. A good _____ setting encourages students to learn and grow.

24. A _____ is a nerve cell.

Environmental Factors Affecting Your Identity

Activity F

Name _____

Section 1:3

Date _____ **Period** _____

In each situation below, identify the environmental factor impacting growth and development.

___J___ 1. Billy hits his sister after watching a violent TV show.

___F___ 2. Tanya's parents expect her to drive her younger brother to school.

___G___ 3. Kim attends a party with friends even though she knows alcohol will be served there.

___A___ 4. Cassie's low level of mental functioning could be traced to her mother's drug use during pregnancy.

___E___ 5. Melissa is expected to buy her own clothing with the money she earns because finances are tight in her single-parent family.

___I___ 6. Zoe was one of the quadruplets conceived in a petri dish and implanted in her mother.

___D___ 7. Sky's family celebrates special events with her grandparents, aunts, uncles, and cousins.

___B___ 8. Rosita learned the alphabet in preschool with other children her age.

___H___ 9. Micah and his family meet often with their friends from church.

___C___ 10. Reggie's favorite subject is physical education, and he enjoys participating in team competitions.

Environmental Factors

A. prenatal environment

B. preschool environment

C. elementary school environment

D. family's cultural heritage

E. family structure

F. sibling position

G. peer influence

H. religion

I. technology

J. media

11. List the environmental factors that had a major influence on your identity. Explain briefly how each factor has influenced your identity. **(Student response.)** _____

_____

_____

_____

_____

_____

_____

_____

_____

Chapter 2

Your Growth and Development

Imagining Self in the Future

Activity A

Section 2:1

Name _____

Date _____   Period _____

Picture what you will be like in the years ahead. In the space provided, list words describing yourself in 4, 10, and 30 years. **(Student response.)**

1. How do you perceive your physical appearance?

   In 4 years   In 10 years   In 30 years

   _____   _____   _____

   _____   _____   _____

   _____   _____   _____

2. What talents and skills will you have developed?

   In 4 years   In 10 years   In 30 years

   _____   _____   _____

   _____   _____   _____

   _____   _____   _____

3. What type of career will you be pursuing?

   In 4 years   In 10 years   In 30 years

   _____   _____   _____

   _____   _____   _____

   _____   _____   _____

4. What relationships will be important to you?

   In 4 years   In 10 years   In 30 years

   _____   _____   _____

   _____   _____   _____

   _____   _____   _____

5. How does your image of yourself today differ from that 4 years from now? 30 years from now?
   (Student response.) _____

   _____

Personal Growth to Maturity

Activity B   Name _____

Section 2:1   Date _____ Period _____

1. In your own words, list the qualities you think would describe an immature person. *(Sample answers:) self-centered, untruthful, irresponsible, unaccepting of others*

_____

_____

_____

2. List four characteristics of a person who is intellectually mature. *(List four:) uses abstract ideas; connects ideas in logical manner; judges the strength or weakness of a viewpoint; able to imagine the self in the future, able to make projections about future consequences*

_____

_____

3. Describe two characteristics of an emotionally mature person. *(Describe two:) develops a close relationship with at least one significant adult, reduces stress in his or her life, avoids use of alcohol and drugs, focuses on learning new skills that help him or her experience success*

_____

_____

4. List four characteristics of a person who is socially mature. *(List four:) considers others' viewpoints; able to share with others, able to consider others' thoughts and feelings, cooperates with others to complete a task, able to give and take in a relationship*

_____

_____

_____

5. Describe six characteristics of a person who has strength in character. *(List six:) follows moral principles—can judge what is right and wrong; is self-disciplined—can control behavior; is dependable—can be counted on; is responsible—answers for his or her behavior and obligations; has integrity—is honest; is motivated to do the best job; has a sense of mercy and justice—seeks to uphold the law*

_____

_____

_____

_____

(Continued)

6. Give an example of how intellectual maturity (or lack of it) might affect a person's success.

    A. On the job: (Sample answer:) With intellectual maturity, people are able to make good decisions and think through their actions. This helps them do well in their jobs.

    B. In a marriage: (Sample answer:) With intellectual maturity, people are able to make good decisions and think through their actions. This helps them make good decisions in a marriage, which makes the marriage stronger.

7. Give an example of how a socially immature person might respond or act.

    A. On the job: (Sample answers:) A socially immature person might arrive late, not call in to report an absence from work, sexually harass another employee, steal from the employer, leave early, and not complete his or her work.

    B. In a marriage: (Sample answers:) A socially immature person might be inflexible, uncooperative with group tasks, unable to share personal thoughts with anyone, and insistent on having his or her own way.

8. Give an example of how emotional maturity (or lack of it) could affect a person's success.

    A. On the job: (Sample answers:) An emotionally immature person may lack self-confidence in his or her abilities, anger easily, talk about other employees behind their backs, get into arguments or fights, or put down another person in order to feel better.

    B. In a marriage: (Sample answers:) A person who is emotionally immature will have a hard time sharing deep and inner feelings, developing an intimate relationship, solving problems without getting angry, and losing control of emotions. Such a marriage may be full of conflict and hostility.

9. Consider your personal qualities on a continuum, with low levels of maturity at one end and high levels at the other end.

    Low Level of Maturity ～～～ **High Level of Maturity**

    A. How do you think your life relates to this continuum? At certain times, a person responds with greater maturity.

    B. Do you think a person is always mature or always immature? Explain your reasoning. (Student response.)

    C. What are some situations in which behaving immaturely could devastate or destroy a person's chance for success? (Sample answer:) If a person responds with immaturity most of the time, it may be difficult to succeed on the job, in a marriage, and in a family. A person's immaturity may cause a loss of a job or a breakdown in a marriage.

My Roles

Name_____

Date _____ Period _____

In the sections below, describe five different roles you have. Then illustrate each role with pictures.

(Student response.)

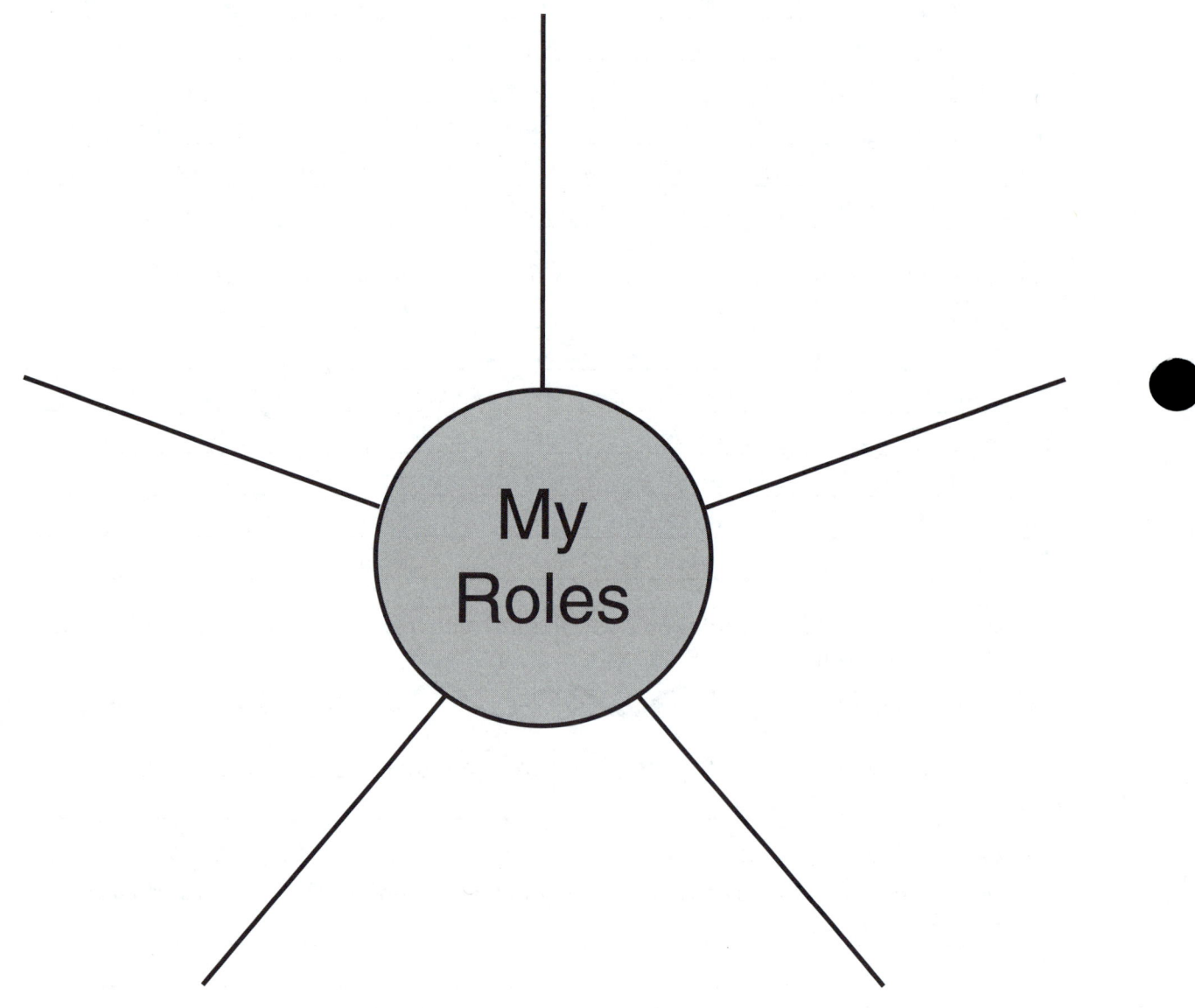

A Checklist for a Self-Study of Character Traits

Activity D

Section 2:1

Name _____

Date _____ Period _____

Use the questions below to examine your character traits. After reading each question, circle the response that most closely describes you. Then answer the final question.

(Student response.)

U–Usually
S–Sometimes
R–Rarely

Self-Discipline	1. Do I accomplish what I plan to do?	U	S	R
	2. Can I say no to myself?	U	S	R
	3. Do I keep myself neat, clean, and appropriately dressed?	U	S	R
Dependability	4. Do I arrive on time for a date or appointment?	U	S	R
	5. Can I be counted on to get a job done?	U	S	R
Responsibility	6. Do I do my share of work when assigned to a group project?	U	S	R
	7. Do I feel that I have a part in helping others grow to their potential?	U	S	R
	8. Do I carry out my jobs without being reminded?	U	S	R
Moral Principles	9. Do I respect others' rights and privileges?	U	S	R
	10. Do I obey the law?	U	S	R
Integrity	11. Do I try to be honest?	U	S	R
	12. Do I present a truthful picture?	U	S	R
Motivation	13 Do I believe that hard work is useful and worthwhile?	U	S	R
	14. Am I enthusiastic about my work?	U	S	R
	15. Do I find satisfaction in doing a job well?	U	S	R
Sense of Mercy and Justice	16. Do I feel compassion when others are ill-treated?	U	S	R
	17. Do I help when I see others in need?	U	S	R
	18. Am I able to look beyond my own desires to consider the welfare of others?	U	S	R

After completing the above checklist, identify specific areas in which you would like to encourage growth. (Focus on your *Sometimes* and *Rarely* responses.) What plan of action will you follow to achieve growth in these areas? Include your specific steps. Whom will you ask to help you be accountable for following your plan? (Student response.) _____

_____

_____

_____

Evaluating Your Self-Concept

Activity E   Name_____

Section 2:2   Date _____ Period _____

Explain the meaning of *self-concept* and follow the directions on both pages to evaluate yours.

1. Define *self-concept*. **Self-concept is the mental picture you have of yourself.**
   _____
   _____

2. Describe what it means to have positive self-esteem. **You have a positive self-concept, feel**
   good about yourself, accept yourself as a worthwhile person, and accept both your strengths
   and weaknesses.
   _____

3. Explain how a person's self-concept can affect feelings of worth and importance, or self-esteem.
   If you have a positive self-concept, you will feel you have worth and value, or high
   self-esteem. If you have a negative self-concept, you may feel worthless and not important,
   having low self-esteem.
   _____
   _____

4. Three factors influence the development of self-concept. Under each factor, describe the way
   you see yourself.

Physical Traits	Skills and Talents	Responses from Others
(Student response.)	**(Student response.)**	**(Student response.)**
_____	_____	_____
_____	_____	_____
_____	_____	_____

5. How could a person's self-concept affect what he or she accomplishes in life? **(Sample response:)**
   A person who has a positive self-concept believes that he or she can accomplish something
   in life, set higher goals, and take action to reach the goals.
   _____
   _____

The statements on the next page identify thoughts and feelings that people with positive self-
concepts may have about themselves. To evaluate your own self-concept, read each statement. Then
circle the number indicating your response. Use the guidelines at the end of the page to evaluate
your responses.

(Continued)

Name_____

	True	Sometimes True	Rarely True
6. I enjoy getting up in the morning.	3	2	1
7. I am usually in a good mood.	3	2	1
8. Most people like me.	3	2	1
9. I usually have a lot of energy.	3	2	1
10. I like the way I look.	3	2	1
11. Others think I am attractive.	3	2	1
12. I am happy with my friends.	3	2	1
13. I can laugh at my mistakes.	3	2	1
14. I look at the positive side of events.	3	2	1
15. I enjoy what I do.	3	2	1
16. I am continuing to grow and change.	3	2	1
17. I am a unique individual.	3	2	1
18. I am kind to others.	3	2	1
19. Others like to have me with them.	3	2	1
20. Others who are close to me care about my opinions.	3	2	1
21. I can tell others how I feel.	3	2	1
22. I can talk easily with others.	3	2	1
23. I plan to do something important in life.	3	2	1
24. My life is interesting.	3	2	1

After completing the activity, add the number of circled responses in each column. A total score closer to 60 shows a high, positive self-concept. A score closer to 40 shows a self-concept high in some areas and low in others. A score closer to 20 shows a low, negative self-concept.

To develop a more positive self-concept, look at each statement to which you responded *Rarely True*. Then answer the following questions:

25. What steps could I take to improve my feelings about this area? (Student response.) _____

_____

_____

26. What skills could I develop to help myself? (Student response.) _____

_____

_____

27. What messages could I give myself to help feel more positive about this area? (Student response.)

_____

_____

Identifying Your Temperament

Activity F   Name_____

Section 2:2   Date _____   Period _____

The statements below list several characteristics relating to various response patterns. To identify some of your response patterns, read each statement. Then check your most immediate response. Evaluate your responses using the guidelines that follow the statements, then answer the questions on the next page.

(Student response.)

	Usually True	Don't Know	Mostly False
1. I often do several tasks at the same time.	_____	_____	_____
2. In comparison with most people I know, I am fairly easygoing.	_____	_____	_____
3. I ordinarily work quickly and energetically.	_____	_____	_____
4. I usually do not plan more work than I can finish.	_____	_____	_____
5. I persist at working on a problem even though it seems overwhelming.	_____	_____	_____
6. I am a good listener and hear people out.	_____	_____	_____
7. I am often in a hurry.	_____	_____	_____
8. I am relaxed when I work.	_____	_____	_____
9. I become impatient when someone slows up in front of me.	_____	_____	_____
10. I feel bothered when people rush me.	_____	_____	_____
11. In conversation with others, I often gesture with my hands.	_____	_____	_____
12. Most people consider me quiet.	_____	_____	_____
13. I really like challenges.	_____	_____	_____
14. I like to eat slowly and enjoy my meals.	_____	_____	_____
15. I walk quickly.	_____	_____	_____
16. I usually can wait patiently.	_____	_____	_____
17. Sometimes I speak too quickly and put words in another person's mouth.	_____	_____	_____
18. I usually speak more softly than most people.	_____	_____	_____
19. I often try to persuade others to my point of view.	_____	_____	_____
20. I usually do not worry about being late.	_____	_____	_____

Total your *Usually True* responses for odd-numbered questions: _____

Next, total your *Usually True* responses for even-numbered questions: _____

If your total number of *Usually True* responses is highest for the odd-numbered questions, your response pattern may be described as hard-driving, impatient, and competitive. (The highest total possible is 10.)

(Continued)

If your total number of *Usually True* responses is highest for even-numbered questions, your response pattern may be described as calm, quiet, relaxed, and easygoing.

21. How would you describe your general behavior patterns?

   A. Physical: (Student response.)
   _____

   B. Intellectual: (Student response.)
   _____

   C. Social: (Student response.)
   _____

   D. Emotional: (Student response.)
   _____

   E. Overall: (Student response.)
   _____

22. Compare these patterns with your parents' patterns. Are there similarities? Are there differences?
   (Student response.)
   _____
   _____
   _____
   _____

23. Explain how these similarities or differences could be both hereditary and environmental.
   (Student response.)
   _____
   _____
   _____
   _____

24. Are there some situations in which you may respond differently, not in a manner that would be natural for you? (Student response.)
   _____
   _____
   _____
   _____

25. How does your environment sometimes cause you to act differently than you naturally would?
   (Student response.)
   _____
   _____

Your Growth and Development

Activity G Name ______________________________

Section 2:2 Date ______________ Period ______________

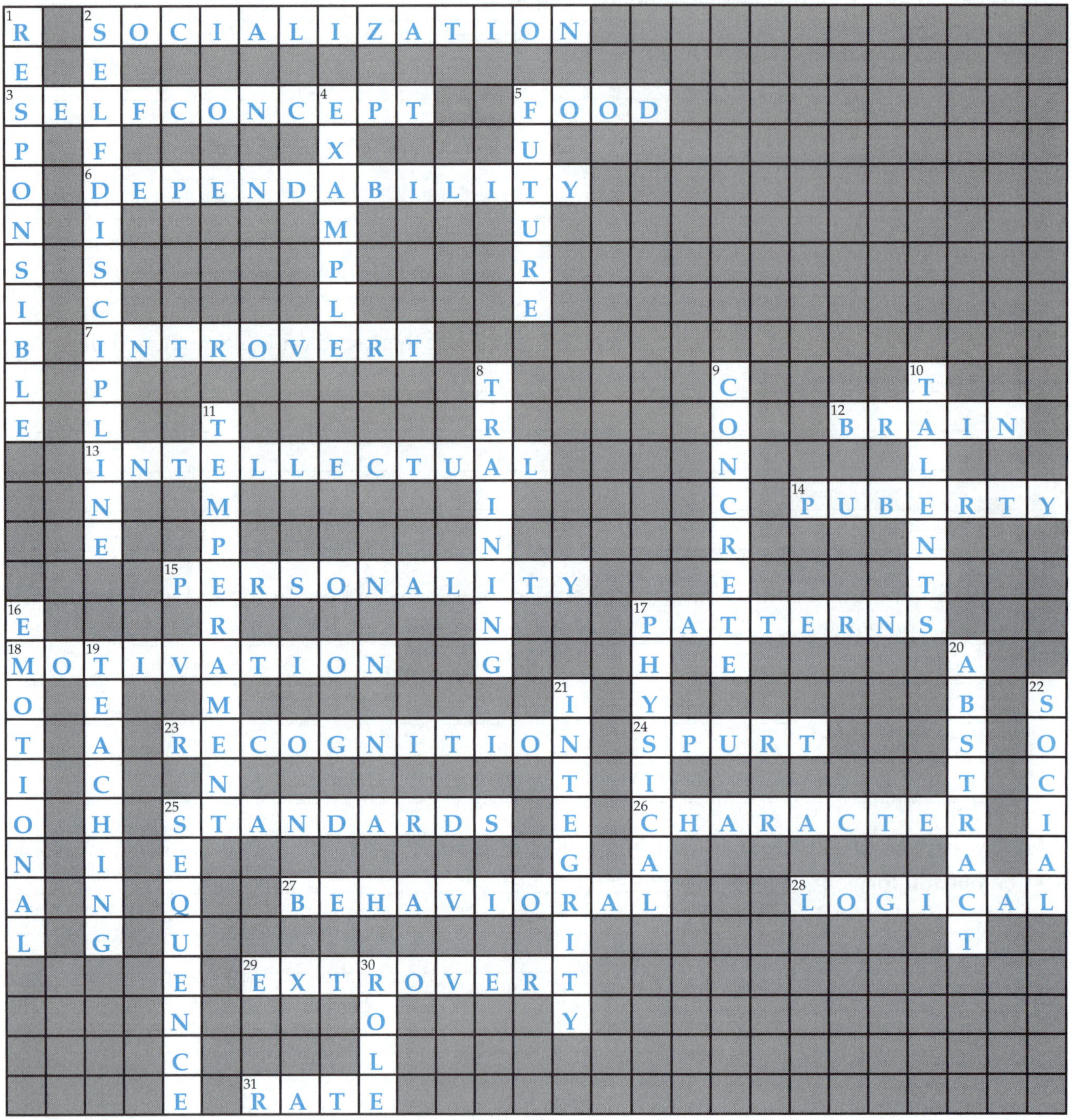

1 RESPONSIBLE
2 SOCIALIZATION
2 SELFDISCIPLINE
3 SELFCONCEPT
4 EXAMPLE
5 FOOD
5 FUTURE
6 DEPENDABILITY
7 INTROVERT
8 TRAINING
9 CONCRETE
10 TALENTS
11 TEMPERAMENT
12 BRAIN
13 INTELLECTUAL
14 PUBERTY
15 PERSONALITY
16 EMOTIONAL
17 PATTERNS
17 PHYSICAL
18 MOTIVATION
19 TEACHING
20 ABSTRACT
21 INTEGRITY
22 SOCIAL
23 RECOGNITION
24 SPURT
25 STANDARDS
25 SEQUENCE
26 CHARACTER
27 BEHAVIORAL
28 LOGICAL
29 EXTROVERT
30 ROLE
31 RATE

(Continued)

Read the descriptions and decide which chapter terms are being described. Write the correct terms in the crossword puzzle.

Across

2. The way you learn behavior that is acceptable in a society.

3. The mental picture you have of yourself is _____-_____.

5. People have physical needs for _____, clothing, and shelter.

6. A character trait that means you are reliable.

7. A person who likes to be alone.

12. Intellectual development refers to the growth of the _____.

13. A growth pattern in which mental activity develops.

14. The time when a growth spurt causes reproductive organs to mature.

15. The sum of all your traits.

17. Growth follows certain _____ in four areas.

18. A drive that moves a person to do a task.

23. People have a need for _____ from others in order to feel successful and capable.

24. Adolescents experience a growth _____ around age 11.

25. Ethics are moral principles or _____ used to judge right and wrong.

26. Your personal judge for every situation you face.

27. Personality is the sum of all personal and _____ traits.

28. Mature people use abstract ideas in a _____ manner.

29. A person who is outgoing.

31. Each person has his or her own _____ of development.

Down

1. A character trait in which you take care of your obligations.

2. The ability to control your behavior is _____-_____.

4. Parents teach children by _____ when they model desired behavior for children to imitate.

5. Mature people can use logic and visualize the _____.

8. Families reinforce their teaching through _____.

9. _____ thinking is related to specific objects.

10. Self-concept is influenced by personal traits, responses from others, and skills and _____.

11. Inborn patterns of response or behavior.

16. An area of growth related to understanding mature feelings.

17. _____ development refers to the growth of the body.

19. One way to learn character traits is through direct _____ by parents.

20. _____ ideas refer to things you cannot see or touch.

21. A character trait meaning honesty.

22. An area of growth related to the development of relationships.

25. Growth patterns follow an orderly _____.

30. A _____ is a way of acting to fulfill certain responsibilities.

Chapter 3

Strengthening Positive Attitudes

Attitude Cycle

Activity A

Name _____

Section 3:1

Date _____ **Period** _____

1. Think of an experience that left you with entirely positive or negative feelings. Describe the events that took place. **(Student response.)** _____
   _____
   _____
   _____

2. What thoughts did you have about the experience? **(Student response.)** _____
   _____
   _____
   _____

3. Were those thoughts positive, negative, or mixed? Explain. **(Student response.)** _____
   _____
   _____
   _____

4. Think of how you responded to the experience. List the actions you took. **(Student response.)**
   _____
   _____
   _____

5. Evaluate how your thoughts about the experience affected your actions. **(Student response.)**
   _____
   _____
   _____

6. Did your actions cause additional positive or negative thoughts? Explain. **(Student response.)**
   _____
   _____
   _____

Defense Mechanisms

Activity B   Name _____

Section 3:1   Date _____ Period _____

Defense mechanisms are methods people unconsciously use to deal with life situations. In each of the following situations, identify the defense mechanism used. Then answer the related questions.

Case 1

Sam's calculus grades were slipping. He could not pass the tests. He studied and worked hard, but forgot small details that resulted in errors when taking the test. He failed the class. Sam was upset and accused his counselor of giving him poor advice. He felt it was the counselor's fault that he failed because the counselor had advised him to take the class.

1. What defense mechanism was Sam using? projection—placing the blame on someone else

_____

_____

2. How could Sam respond to this situation in a way that would help him grow as a person? (Sample answers:) have realistic expectations, set realistic goals, seek career counseling to assess his skills and aptitudes and a good career match for them

_____

_____

Case 2

Roberta's parents spent years helping her acquire basketball skills. They sent her to special training camps and practiced with her in the evenings. They expected her to win a college basketball scholarship like her older sister, but Roberta preferred to play music. She wanted to play in the jazz band that was held after school, but her parents convinced her to stay with basketball. When she was not offered a scholarship, her parents became upset and accused her of not working hard enough.

3. What defense mechanism was being used? idealization—valuing something more than it is worth

_____

4. How could her parents' expectations affect Roberta's self-esteem? The parents' expectations could result in poor self-esteem for Roberta since she could not live up to them.

_____

_____

5. What could Roberta do in this situation to help herself grow as a person and build self-esteem? (Sample answers:) set realistic goals for herself, explain the goals she sets for her life to her parents

_____

_____

Building Positive Attitudes

Activity C

Name _____

Section 3:1

Date _____ **Period** _____

Negative mental attitudes are often learned. They may result from low self-esteem, unrealistic expectations, living with criticism, or lack of success in various situations. Using defense mechanisms to deal with these feelings may limit personal growth. Building a positive attitude is a healthful way to help yourself grow to maturity. Respond to the statements below to help evaluate and improve your own mental attitudes.

1. I feel inferior when (Student response.) _____

   _____

   _____

   _____

   _____

2. I usually respond to these situations by (Student response.) _____

   _____

   _____

   _____

   _____

3. Identify ways you could use the following techniques to build positive feelings and attitudes:

   Direct attack:
   I could change (Student response.) _____

   _____

   Compensation:
   I could (Student response.) _____ to compensate for _____

   _____

   Reasonable expectations:
   I could plan (Student response.) _____

   _____

   Positive self-talk:
   I could say (Student response.) _____ when _____

   _____

   Interpretation of facts:
   I could think (Student response.) _____ when _____

   _____

   Friendship choices:
   I could select friends who (Student response.) _____

   _____

Sources of Stress

You will likely experience some type of stress every day. The more sources of stress you experience at one time, the greater the effects of the stress will be. Use the following questions to help you identify some sources of stress and actions you can take to manage stress.

1. What are five situations that have caused you stress recently?
   A. (Student response.) _____
   B. (Student response.) _____
   C. (Student response.) _____
   D. (Student response.) _____
   E. (Student response.) _____

2. How did the stress affect you in each situation?
   A. (Student response.) _____
   B. (Student response.) _____
   C. (Student response.) _____
   D. (Student response.) _____
   E. (Student response.) _____

3. What was the source of the stress in each situation? Was it normal or crisis-producing stress?

Source of Stress	Normal or Crisis-Producing?
A. (Chart answers are student response.)	
B.	
C.	
D.	
E.	

Choose one of the situations above, circle it, and answer the following questions.

4. What action can you take to remove the source of the stress? (Student response.) _____

_____

_____

_____

_____

(Continued)

5. What action can you take to remove yourself from the stressful situation? **(Student response.)** _____

_____

_____

6. How can you change your response to the stress? **(Student response.)** _____

_____

_____

7. Can you manage the stress by focusing on one part at a time? If so, which part? **(Student response.)** _____

_____

_____

8. Stress can result in attitudes such as anger, anxiety, and depression. These attitudes need to be handled and resolved or they will result in continued negative attitudes that will impact your life. List some stressors in your life that might cause the following:

Anger	Anxiety	Depression
(Student response.)	**(Student response.)**	**(Student response.)**
_____	_____	_____
_____	_____	_____

9. What actions could you take to reduce feelings of anger? Consider the four different ways to handle stressors. **(Student response.)** _____

_____

_____

10. What actions could you take to handle feelings of anxiety? **(Student response.)** _____

_____

_____

11. What steps could you take to handle feelings of depression? **(Student response.)** _____

_____

_____

_____

Stress Management and Positive Attitudes

Activity E

Section 3:2

Name _____

Date _____ Period _____

This activity will help you develop skills in managing stress in your life. Reducing stress and its negative effects can help you keep positive attitudes. Use the following questions and statements to guide you. Choose one stressful situation and then identify a plan to manage the stress and reduce its effects.

1. Identify a stressful situation in your life. Describe it and identify its cause or source. (Student response.)

   _____

   _____

   _____

2. What can you do to manage this situation? List your possible alternatives. Include at least three, if you can.

   A. (Student response.) _____

   B. (Student response.) _____

   C. (Student response.) _____

3. Consider the pros and cons of each alternative.

   A. (Student response.) _____

   B. (Student response.) _____

   C. (Student response.) _____

4. Choose the alternative that will be most effective for you and develop a plan to carry it out.
   (Student response.) _____

   _____

   _____

   _____

5. Describe how you will evaluate your effectiveness in managing the stress and reducing its negative effects on you. (Student response.) _____

   _____

   _____

   _____

   _____

Strengthening Positive Attitudes

Activity F

Section 3:2

Name _____

Date _____ Period _____

Complete the statements about attitudes by filling in the blanks.

__Attitudes__

1. _____ are learned behaviors that people develop through interaction with their environment.

__Mental health__

2. _____ _____ is the overall condition of a person's attitudes.

__projection__

3. Placing the blame for personal failures on others is called _____.

__Displacement__

4. _____ is when people take out their feelings on someone or something else rather than face the real problem.

__perpetuating__

5. The cycle of attitudes producing actions that cause the attitudes to increase is called a self-_____ cycle.

__conversion__

6. Transferring an emotion into a physical symptom is called _____.

__regression__

7. Returning to childish or immature behavior when difficulties or frustrations occur is called _____.

__Idealization__

8. _____ is valuing someone or something far more than the true worth.

__mechanisms__

9. People who cover up or hide negative feelings may use defense _____ rather than admit a weakness or failure.

__rationalization__

10. When people make socially acceptable excuses for their behaviors, they are using _____.

__fantasy__

11. When people use their imagination to fill personal needs, they are using _____ as a defense mechanism.

__direct__

12. Positive attitudes can be built by _____ attack, during which a person faces a problem and tries to solve it.

__compensation__

13. With _____, people try to make up for a weakness by emphasizing an area in which they can succeed.

__self-talk__

14. Little messages you send to yourself are called _____-_____.

__normative__

15. Normal events that you experience on a daily basis and cause stress are called _____ stressors.

__crises__

16. Major events that cause a lot of stress and require major changes in your life are called _____ events.

__Stress__

17. _____ is the body's response to the events of life that cause physical, mental, and emotional tensions.

__Sex stereotypes__

18. _____ _____ are widely held beliefs about the characteristics shared by all men or all women.

(Continued)

_____Normal_____ 19. _____ anxiety occurs when a person recognizes a threat and does something to remove the threat.

_____anxiety_____ 20. The uneasy feeling in a person's mind that something terrible is going to happen is called _____.

_____Depression_____ 21. _____ is an overwhelming attitude of sadness, discouragement, and hopelessness.

_____roles_____ 22. Sex _____ are the society's definition of how males and females should behave.

_____stereotype_____ 23. A(n) _____ is an oversimplified opinion or prejudiced attitude.

_____High_____ 24. _____ anxiety keeps people from acting in ways that correct the problem.

Chapter 4

Developing Decision-Making Skills

Discovering Your Personal Values and Goals

Activity A   Name _____

Section 4:1   Date _____ Period _____

1. List the ideals or beliefs that are important to you in each of the following areas.

Personal Areas	Relationship Areas	Work Areas
(Chart answers are student response.)		

2. Considering your answers above, list what you would like to accomplish in life in each area. These plans become your goals.

Personal Goals	Relationship Goals	Work Goals
(Chart answers are student response.)		

Reaching Your Goals

Activity B   Name _____

Section 4:1   Date _____   Period _____

Choose one major life goal from your list in Activity A. Develop a plan of action to help you reach your goal.

(Chart answers are student response.)

Goal: _____   Desired deadline: _____

Plan of Action	
Subgoal: _____	Completion Date: _____
Steps: 1. 2. 3. 4.	
Subgoal: _____	Completion Date: _____
Steps: 1. 2. 3. 4.	
Possible Obstacles: _____ _____ _____	**Trade-Offs I May Need to Make:** _____ _____ _____

What standards can you identify to help you measure your progress in reaching this goal?
(Student response.)

_____

_____

_____

_____

_____

Identify Your Resources

Activity C

Name_____

Section 4:1

Date _____ Period _____

Using the words listed at the bottom of the page, fill in the blanks below. Identify various human and nonhuman resources that a person could use to help carry out a decision. Each word is used once.

Human Resources

A. Personal:

1. Physical and mental resources: ____**energy**____, ____**experience**____, ____**good health**____, ____**knowledge**____, ____**strength**____

2. Personality traits: ____**artistic**____, ____**friendly**____, ____**inquisitive**____, ____**nervous**____, ____**outgoing**____, ____**temperamental**____

3. Character traits: ____**dependable**____, ____**honest**____, ____**moral**____, ____**reliable**____, ____**responsible**____

4. Skills and abilities: ____**conversing**____, ____**cooking**____, ____**decision making**____, ____**playing an instrument**____, ____**problem solving**____, ____**reading**____, ____**writing**____

B. Other human resources: ____**family members**____, ____**friends**____, ____**religious leader**____, ____**teachers**____

Nonhuman Resources

A. Money: ____**allowance**____, ____**paycheck**____, ____**savings**____

B. Personal Possessions: ____**car**____, ____**clothes**____, ____**computer**____

C. Community Resources: ____**parks**____, ____**schools**____, ____**stores**____, ____**zoo**____

D. Information: ____**books**____, ____**database**____, ____**Internet**____, ____**magazines**____

E. 24 hours per day: ____**time**____

allowance	energy	moral	savings
artistic	experience	nervous	schools
books	family members	outgoing	stores
car	friendly	parks	strength
clothes	friends	paycheck	teachers
computer	good health	playing an instrument	temperamental
conversing	honest	problem solving	time
cooking	inquisitive	reading	writing
database	Internet	reliable	zoo
decision making	knowledge	religious leader	
dependable	magazines	responsible	

Steps in the Decision-Making Process

Activity D   Name _____

Section 4:2   Date _____ Period _____

Use the information on the decision-making process in your text to complete the activity.

1. List the six steps in the decision-making process.

    A. Identify the decision to be made. _____

    B. Identify the alternatives. _____

    C. Consider each alternative. _____

    D. Choose the best alternative. _____

    E. Carry out the decision. _____

    F. Evaluate the decision. _____

2. You will be graduating from high school in the near future. List 10 decisions related to this life
    event that you will need to make. **(The following are sample answers.)**

    A. choose a career pathway _____

    B. choose a career _____

    C. choose colleges to which to apply _____

    D. how to obtain money for college _____

    E. a place to live _____

    F. what part-time job will not interfere with school _____

    G. how to manage my money _____

    H. whether to buy a car _____

    I. what type of car insurance to get _____

3. Identify which step of the decision-making process is completed in each of the following activities.

Activity	Step in the Decision-Making Process
1. Take a career inventory.	Identify the decision to be made.
2. Sign up for classes at the college you have chosen.	Carry out the decision.
3. Visit two different colleges.	Consider each alternative.
4. Talk to students who have attended colleges in which you are interested.	Consider each alternative.
5. Identify whether you had enough information to make a good decision.	Evaluate the decision.
6. Search the Internet for colleges that prepare students for the career in which you are interested.	Identify the alternatives.
7. Consider the colleges that have accepted your application and choose one to attend.	Choose the best alternative.
8. Compare what different colleges have to offer by investigating their Web sites.	Consider each alternative.

Chapter 5

Developing Communication Skills

Nonverbal Communication

Activity A   Name _____

Section 5:1   Date _____ Period _____

In the space provided, answer the following questions about using different forms of nonverbal communication to send messages.

1. Nonverbal communication can be described as <u>any message communicated without words</u>
   _____

2. List three different facial expressions. Then describe the meanings they may convey to the receiver.
   <u>(List three:) furrowed brow—concern, upset, worry, disagree; smile—happy, content; eye</u>
   <u>contact—shows interest, care, concern; and raised eyebrows—questioning</u>
   _____

3. List three different body motions. Then describe the meanings they may convey to the receiver.
   <u>(List three:) sitting forward—alert, listening; slouching—disinterest; crossing legs—</u>
   <u>relaxed; crossing arms—sets up a barrier; good posture—confidence</u>
   _____

4. Describe two forms of touch that could be used in a job situation to provide encouragement
   and give a person positive feedback on completing a task. <u>(List two:) a light touch on the</u>
   <u>arm, pat on the back, or firm handshake</u>
   _____

5. What forms of touch would be considered unacceptable on the job or in a work environment?
   Explain your answer. <u>Sexually interpreted forms of touch such as a kiss or hug may be</u>
   <u>viewed by others as too personal.</u>
   _____

6. How can learning about nonverbal communication help you communicate more effectively?
   <u>(Student response.)</u>
   _____
   _____

The Self-Awareness Circle

Activity B

Name _____

Section 5:1

Date _____ **Period** _____

1. Describe a situation that affected you strongly in some way. **(Student response.)** _____

   _____

   _____

   _____

   _____

   _____

2. Using the circle below, express your point of view about that situation. Using I-statements, record your personal observations, thoughts, feelings, intentions, and actions on the circle.
   (Student response.)

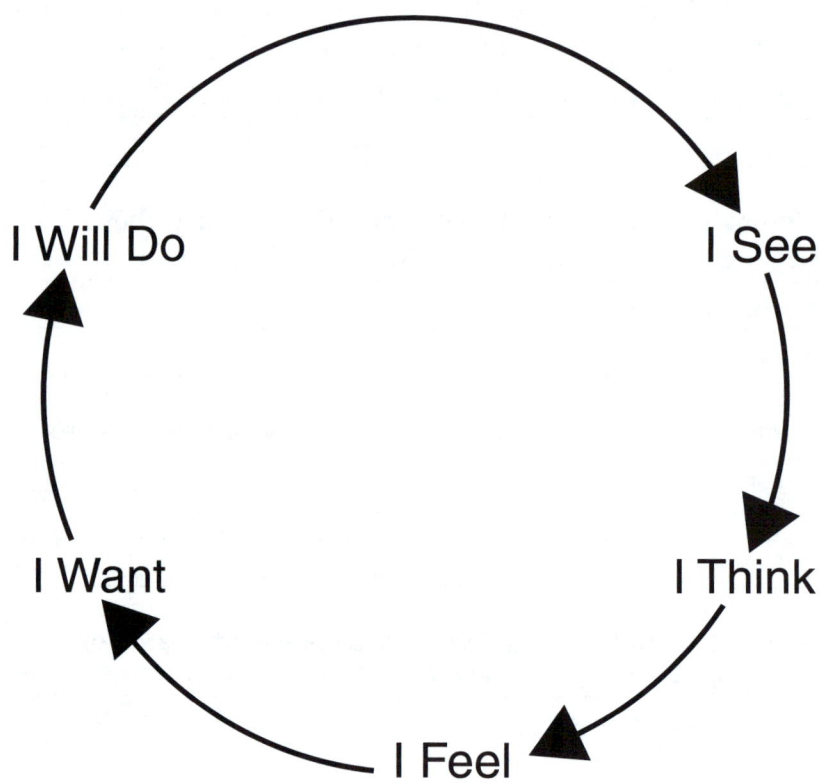

I Will Do

I See

I Want

I Think

I Feel

Using I-Statements to Speak for Yourself

Activity C

Name _____

Section 5:1

Date _____ **Period** _____

For each of the following situations, write an I-statement that expresses your point of view (observations, thoughts, feelings, desires, intended action, or a combination of these).

1. You are dining with friends at a restaurant that offers an all-you-can-eat salad bar. You would like more salad, but the server fails to ask you if you would like a clean plate. **(Student response.)** _____

_____

_____

_____

_____

_____

_____

2. At an all-school assembly, your friend is making rude and impolite comments to the person sitting in front of you. This bothers you, and you want your friend to stop. **(Student response.)** _____

_____

_____

_____

_____

_____

_____

3. A good friend wants to borrow your car, but you do not want to lend it. **(Student response.)** _____

_____

_____

_____

_____

_____

_____

4. At school, a student in the hall makes a cutting remark to you about your choice of clothing. **(Student response.)**

_____

_____

_____

_____

_____

You-Statements: Responses to Avoid

Name_____

Date _____ Period _____

Imagine that each of the following you-statements is told to you in response to your revealing a personal problem to a friend. Describe how the messages might make you feel. (Some possible descriptors could include *defensive, resistant, inadequate, inferior, labeled,* and *worthless.*)

1. You shouldn't say things like that.
   (Student response.)
   _____

   _____

2. You'll feel better about it tomorrow. Things always turn out.
   (Student response.)
   _____

   _____

3. Just forget about it. Ignore him.
   (Student response.)
   _____

   _____

4. You're so dumb. Can't you be more responsible?
   (Student response.)
   _____

   _____

5. You always bring up the same old problem. Do we have to talk about this again?
   (Student response.)
   _____

   _____

6. You think you're always right. You never make a mistake!
   (Student response.)
   _____

   _____

7. I think you let things bother you too much.
   (Student response.)
   _____

   _____

8. Let's just forget about it.
   (Student response.)
   _____

   _____

9. You always ignore me.
   (Student response.)
   _____

   _____

10. Why did you spend your money on that?
    (Student response.)
    _____

    _____

Barriers to Communication

Name _____

Date _____   Period _____

Match the following examples to the communication barrier being described or used.

Barriers to Communication

___D___ 1. I will not talk to a Democrat (or Republican).

___A___ 2. I'm not going down that hallway where the popular group hangs out.

___F___ 3. All teens are irresponsible.

___G___ 4. Only men can be good mechanics.

___B___ 5. I hate that nickname.

___C___ 6. Let's talk this over at the dance.

___E___ 7. She can't be a leader in this community if she attends that church.

___G___ 8. I really didn't think you would be a good math partner, being a girl.

___D___ 9. I've already decided that I will never eat at that restaurant.

A. low self-esteem
B. intense emotion
C. noisy environment
D. closed minds
E. religious prejudice
F. age prejudice
G. gender prejudice

10. If a person you were speaking with used the above statements, how would you, as a listener, feel? **(Sample answer:) The comments would not make me feel like talking with the person.**

_____

_____

11. How could these comments affect communication? **The comments are barriers to communication. Communication would be poor because the barriers prevent the sender and receiver from thinking clearly about the real message.**

_____

12. Describe a time when you experienced a barrier to communication. Explain the factors that caused a breakdown in communication. **(Student response.)** _____

_____

_____

_____

_____

_____

Who Owns the Problem?

Activity F   Name _____

Section 5:3   Date _____ Period _____

For each of the following situations, identify who owns the problem. Then describe the steps the people involved could take to resolve their conflict.

1. Jenna and Katie share a bedroom. Jenna leaves her clothes on the floor and only picks them up when it's time to do laundry. Katie does not like the mess when her friends come over. <u>Katie owns</u> <u>the problem. (Sample answer:) Katie accepts ownership of the problem. She tells Jenna</u> <u>it bothers her that the bedroom is messy when her friends come over. Katie purchases</u> <u>two clothes hampers and suggests that they each put their dirty clothes into the hampers</u> <u>instead of on the floor.</u>

_____

2. Frank's neighbor parks his car so it blocks Frank's driveway. As a result, Frank can't back his own car out to go to school in the morning. <u>Frank owns the problem. (Sample answer:) Frank</u> <u>accepts ownership of the problem. He tells his neighbor that his car is preventing Frank from</u> <u>getting to school in the morning. Frank identifies where the neighbor could park his car so</u> <u>that it doesn't block the driveway and asks the neighbor to park there.</u>

_____

3. The English teacher assigns a group debate. However, two of your team members do not do their share of preparation. They are not ready to debate on your assigned day. <u>Everyone</u> <u>bothered by the problem should take ownership. (Sample answer:) You and a few team</u> <u>members accept ownership of the problem. You ask your teacher if your group can debate</u> <u>the next day because some of your team members did not prepare. You ask the two</u> <u>unprepared team members to make sure they are ready to debate tomorrow.</u>

_____

4. Kari makes plans to drive her friends to a movie Friday night. When she asks her dad for the car, however, she learns that he will need it since he is working late. <u>Kari owns the problem,</u> <u>and if they are bothered by it, her friends. (Sample answer:) Kari accepts ownership of the</u> <u>problem. Kari e-mails everyone who is going to the movie on Friday night. She lets them</u> <u>know that her dad needs the car and asks if someone else can drive.</u>

_____

Communication

A crossword puzzle with the following answers:

1 Across: BODY LANGUAGE
4 Across: SENDER
8 Across: SELF AWARENESS
9 Across: FROWN
10 Across: NEGOTIATION
12 Across: COMMUNICATION
13 Across: CONFLICT
15 Across: DESCRIPTIVE
17 Across: VERBAL
20 Across: REFLECTING
22 Across: SHARED
25 Across: RESOLUTION
27 Across: GESTURES
31 Across: PREJUDICE
32 Across: BLAMING
33 Across: BARRIERS
34 Across: IDENTIFY
35 Across: LEARNED

Down answers (letters visible in grid):

2 Down: YOUSTATEMENTS
3 Down: FEELING
5 Down: DISTRACTING
6 Down: ISTATEMENEN
7 Down: THUGHT
11 Down: REE
14 Down: CWN
16 Down: HEKI
17 Down: VERRS
18 Down: LACTIVE
19 Down: COMPROMIS
21 Down: CONVGROUT AL
23 Down: PACATATT
24 Down: ACTION
26 Down: RCECEI VE
27 Down: G
28 Down: INTENTION
29 Down: MIX
30 Down: PASSIVE

(Continued)

Read the descriptions and decide which chapter terms are being described. Write the correct terms in the crossword puzzle.

Across

1. _____ _____ involves sending messages through body movements.
4. The person who transmits or sends the message.
8. The _____-_____ circle shows how people can use I-statements to express their points of view.
9. A _____ is a facial expression that can show you disagree with what is said.
10. People take turns sending and receiving messages to reach a solution to a problem.
12. An exchange of information between two or more people.
13. When two people disagree on some issue.
15. Statements that report what you have seen or heard.
17. Using words to send and receive messages.
20. Repeating a message in your own words.
22. Good communication occurs when a _____ meaning is reached.
25. A term meaning a conflict is settled.
27. Arm movements used to send messages.
31. Biased opinions formed without complete knowledge or facts.
32. A pattern in which people accuse others for everything that goes wrong.
33. A closed mind, a mixed message, and poor listening skills are examples of communication _____.
34. The first step in solving a problem is to _____ it.
35. Communication skills can be _____.

Down

2. _____-_____ make other people feel put down and inferior.
3. Statements that let others know how you feel.
5. A pattern in which people ignore unpleasant situations.
6. _____-_____ can be used to speak clearly for yourself.
7. Statements that describe your interpretations.
11. A _____ environment helps promote good communication.
14. The second step in problem solving is to identify problem _____.
16. Asking questions to clarify a message is an example of _____-_____.
18. A type of listening in which the receiver responds to the sender.
19. Both parties give in somewhat to reach a solution.
21. The part of a message that is not words.
23. A pattern in which people try to please others.
24. Statements that let others know what you are doing now.
26. The person who hears and interprets the message.
28. Statements that let others know what you want to do.
29. A person sending a _____ message is using body language that doesn't agree with his or her spoken words.
30. _____ listening means just taking in a message.

Chapter 6

Family and Peer Relationships

Am I Friendship Material?

Activity A

Name_____

Section 6:1

Date _____ Period _____

Read each of the following statements. Place a check in the column that best represents your feelings.
(Answers are student response.)

	Usually	Sometimes	Rarely
1. I am friendly.	_____	_____	_____
2. I can accept others.	_____	_____	_____
3. I can accept others' viewpoints even if they are different from mine.	_____	_____	_____
4. I can reveal my feelings to others.	_____	_____	_____
5. I have rapport with others.	_____	_____	_____
6. I like most people.	_____	_____	_____
7. I feel that most people like me.	_____	_____	_____
8. I am honest with others.	_____	_____	_____
9. I have trust in others.	_____	_____	_____
10. I can keep information a secret.	_____	_____	_____
11. I see others as human beings.	_____	_____	_____
12. I can relate person-to-person.	_____	_____	_____
13. I like to benefit others.	_____	_____	_____
14. I like to make other people feel good about themselves.	_____	_____	_____
15. I enjoy rewarding others.	_____	_____	_____
16 I am dependable.	_____	_____	_____
17. I like to learn from others.	_____	_____	_____
18. I am willing to share power with others.	_____	_____	_____

These statements describe qualities that can help people develop close friendships. Take a look at the statements you checked *rarely*. Consider what you can do to improve those areas.

The Impact of Friendships

Activity B   Name _____

Section 6:1   Date _____   Period _____

Answer the questions below. Then read the case study on the next page and answer the questions that follow.

1. List ten individuals that you would consider acquaintances (you at least know their names and they know yours). **(Student response.)** _____

   _____

   _____

2. List three individuals whom you would identify as good friends. **(Student response.)** _____

   _____

   _____

3. List two individuals you would identify as close friends (or best friends). **(Student response.)** ___

   _____

   _____

4. What do you have in common with all the friends you listed above? **(Student response.)** _____

   _____

   _____

5. Why do you think people usually do not identify many close friends? **Close friendships take more time to develop so it's not likely that a person would disclose intimate details to many people.**

   _____

6. What feelings might a person experience if he or she had few friends but felt that others had many? **(Sample answer:) A person may feel inferior or left out.**

   _____

7. How can friendships help a person grow intellectually? **Friendships help a person develop thinking skills and logical reasoning and make clearer projections.**

   _____

8. How can friendships help a person grow emotionally? **Friendships help a person identify emotions, develop empathy, and feel accepted.**

   _____

9. How can friendships help a person grow socially? **Friendships help a person learn to give and take, develop communication skills, and see others' points of view.**

   _____

(Continued)

Case Study

Sitting at the police station, Lolita wondered how she had ever gotten into this situation. She and her boyfriend, Jaffre, were being charged with theft. They had been shopping, and what seemed like an innocent little candy bar taken when they thought no one was looking suddenly became a charge of theft. Her eyes were blurred and she could not think clearly, but she knew she was in trouble. It was her first offense, but to her surprise, Jaffre had a long list of offenses. "How did I get mixed up in this?" she asked herself.

As a newcomer to the school, Lolita had been worried about making new friends. It seemed there were so many small cliques in the school. She could never break into any of them. Her fears, however, were unfounded. Jaffre had taken an interest in her as soon as he saw her. He had introduced himself to her and invited her to hang out with him and his friends. She felt accepted by the group, and they were fun and light-hearted. At first, she thought it strange that Jaffre carried so much cash. She thought it must be nice to have so much money. He shared what he had freely, buying gifts for her and his friends. Sometimes, though, he would run low on cash and ask to borrow some from her. She didn't mind, however, since he was her friend and had spent so much on her. It seemed, though, that neither of them ever had any money lately. She remembered the first party he had taken her to. Not wanting to lose her new friends, she had joined in the marijuana party. She remembered thinking, "Just once won't hurt." Now look where she was.

10. What needs did Lolita have in her life that resulted in her making the choices that she made?
    fear of the unknown, need to be accepted, desire to be included in a group

    _____

    _____

11. Why do you think Jaffre's group of friends were so accepting of Lolita? _She was new, in need_
    of friends, and they had no requirements to join their group other than to participate with
    them in their activities.

    _____

12. What influence did this group of friends have on Lolita's emotional, social, intellectual, and physical growth? _Emotionally they accepted her, which increased her self-esteem. However,_
    since self-esteem is also related to a person's feelings about what he or she can do,
    ultimately, her self-esteem decreased. Physically, they used drugs to dull her mind, which
    inhibited her intellectual growth and kept her from making logical, reasoned decisions.
    Socially, she went along with the group rather than stick to her standards and values.

    _____

13. What suggestions would you have for new students coming into your school to help them make friends that would have a positive impact on their growth and development? _(Student_
    response. Should relate to identifying common interests, values, and goals when choosing
    friends and joining groups.)

    _____

    _____

Let's Get Acquainted

Name_____

Date _____   Period _____

This activity can be done in a small group or with one other person. Each person in the group must answer the same question before moving on to the next question. **(Answers are student response.)**

1. My name is _____ .

2. I live _____ .

3. In my family, there are _____ .

4. My favorite movie/book is _____ .

5. I like to do _____ as a hobby.

6. After high school, I plan to _____ .

7. Other plans I have for the future include: _____ .

8. When I am alone, I like to _____ .

9. I feel _____ about working in small groups.

10. Getting to know new people makes me feel _____ .

11. Most of all, I enjoy _____ about life.

12. I like to daydream about _____ .

13. I most dislike doing _____ .

14. I find it hardest to share with others when I feel _____ .

15. I find it easy to share _____ feelings with others.

16. I think one trait that makes me special is _____ .

17. I am weak in _____ .

18. I feel good about myself when _____ .

19. I am afraid of _____ .

20. A really painful experience for me was when _____ .

These questions have proceeded from general informational topics to personal feelings and ideas about yourself. Sharing at deeper levels can help deeper friendships develop.

How did sharing personal feelings and information make you feel in this setting? **(Student response.)**

_____

_____

Assertiveness Rating Scale

Name _____

Date _____   Period _____

Read the following statements. Some may be very characteristic of you. Others may be very unlike you. For each statement, check the space in one of the three right columns that best describes you.

Complete the blank on the left side by reading the directions below.

		Usually	Sometimes	Rarely
passive	1. I hesitate to make or accept dates because of shyness.	_____	_____	_____
assertive	2. When food served at a restaurant is not done to my satisfaction, I bring it to the server's attention.	_____	_____	_____
passive	3. When a salesperson takes extra time to show merchandise to me, I have a hard time saying no.	_____	_____	_____
aggressive	4. I enjoy a good, vigorous argument.	_____	_____	_____
passive	5. People often take advantage of me.	_____	_____	_____
assertive	6. I strive to get ahead as much as most people I know.	_____	_____	_____
assertive	7. I enjoy starting conversations with people I don't know.	_____	_____	_____
passive	8. Often I don't know what to say to attractive members of the opposite sex.	_____	_____	_____
passive	9. I find it embarrassing to return merchandise.	_____	_____	_____
passive	10. I avoid asking questions for fear of sounding stupid.	_____	_____	_____
passive	11. I avoid making a scene at all costs.	_____	_____	_____
passive	12. When I am given a compliment, I don't know what to say.	_____	_____	_____
assertive	13. I am open about my feelings.	_____	_____	_____
assertive	14. If a couple near me in a theater were talking loudly, I would ask them to be quiet.	_____	_____	_____
assertive	15. I let others know when I have accomplished something worthwhile.	_____	_____	_____

For each of the above statements, identify whether the statement is a *passive*, *aggressive*, or *assertive* response. Then write your response in the blank on the left side. When you are finished, complete the next page. **(Answers are student response.)**

(Continued)

Name_____

1. Total the number of *assertive* responses you marked:

   Usually _____

   Sometimes _____

   Never _____

2. Total the number of *aggressive* responses you marked:

   Usually _____

   Sometimes _____

   Never _____

3. Total the number of *passive* responses you marked:

   Usually _____

   Sometimes _____

   Never _____

4. Summarize with a description of how you most often express yourself. (Student response.) _____

   _____

   _____

   _____

   _____

   _____

   _____

   _____

   _____

   _____

   _____

   _____

   _____

   _____

   _____

   _____

   _____

   _____

   _____

   _____

Family Communication

Name_____

Date _____ Period _____

How well do members in your family know each other? This activity provides a good opportunity for improving family communication. Ask your parent or another significant adult in your family to respond to each of the following questions. Then respond to the questions yourself. After you have finished, compare and discuss each other's responses.   **(Answers are student response.)**

	Adult's Response	Your Response
1.	_____	_____
2.	_____	_____
3.	_____	_____
4.	_____	_____
5.	_____	_____
6.	_____	_____
7.	_____	_____
8.	_____	_____
9.	_____	_____
10.	_____	_____
11.	_____	_____
12.	_____	_____
13.	_____	_____
14.	_____	_____
15.	_____	_____
16.	_____	_____
17.	_____	_____
18.	_____	_____
19.	_____	_____
20.	_____	_____

1. Who is _____ best friend? (Write your name here.)

2. What embarrasses him/her most?

3. What is his/her biggest fear?

4. What is his/her favorite musical group?

5. What person outside the family has influenced his/her life?

6. Of what accomplishment is he/she proudest?

7. What is his/her biggest complaint about the family?

8. What is his/her favorite TV show?

9. What sport does he/she enjoy most?

10. What are his/her favorite subjects in school?

11. Who is his/her favorite teacher?

12. What really makes him/her angry?

13. Does he/she feel liked by others at school?

14. What would he/she like to do when finished with school?

15. What has been his/her biggest disappointment this year?

16. Where would he/she like to go on vacation?

17. What are his/her favorite foods?

18. What nicknames is he/she called at school?

19. When does he/she prefer to do homework?

20. What is his/her most prized possession?

Developing Skills for Work Relationships

Activity F   Name_____

Section 6:3   Date _____   Period _____

The relationship skills in the chart below are identified by the U.S. Department of Labor as important for employees in many careers.* Analyze the degree to which you have developed each skill by writing *beginning*, *somewhat developed*, or *well developed* in the second column. In the third column, identify experiences that could help you develop each skill.

Relationship skills needed	Degree to which you have mastered the skill	Experiences that will help you develop the skill
Active Listening—giving full attention to what other people are saying and responding with feedback	(beginning, somewhat developed, or well developed)	(Student response.)
Speaking—talking to others to convey information effectively	(beginning, somewhat developed, or well developed)	(Student response.)
Instructing—teaching others how to do something	(beginning, somewhat developed, or well developed)	(Student response.)
Coordination—adjusting actions in relation to others' actions	(beginning, somewhat developed, or well developed)	(Student response.)
Negotiation—bringing others together and trying to reconcile differences	(beginning, somewhat developed, or well developed)	(Student response.)
Persuasion—persuading others to change their minds or behaviors	(beginning, somewhat developed, or well developed)	(Student response.)
Service Orientation—actively looking for ways to help people	(beginning, somewhat developed, or well developed)	(Student response.)
Social Perceptiveness—being aware of others' reactions and understanding why they react as they do	(beginning, somewhat developed, or well developed)	(Student response.)

Identify a career that interests you. Explain which relationship skills would be most important to master for future career success. (Student response.) _____

_____

_____

_____

_____

*Reference: http://online.onetcenter.org

Chapter 7

Dating

Functions of Dating

Activity A

Name _____

Section 7:1

Date _____ **Period** _____

The dating process serves many important functions, including those listed below. Read each statement and briefly describe how that dating function may contribute to your overall growth and development. Then give an example for each.

1. Dating can help you get to know others. _(Sample answer:) Dating can help you learn how others think and feel, what they like to do, and what their goals are._ _____

   Example _(Student response.)_ _____

2. Dating can help you get to know yourself. _(Sample answer:) Developing a relationship requires that you share your ideas and feelings. As you share, and the other person reflects back what you say, you learn more about yourself._

   Example _(Student response.)_ _____

3. Dating can provide companionship. _(Sample answer:) Dating gives you the opportunity to spend time with someone who shares your interests._ _____

   Example _(Student response.)_ _____

4. Dating can improve your communication skills. _(Sample answer:) Dating provides opportunities to talk and listen to your dating partner. Open communication is an important part of building any relationship. Dating can help you learn how to send clear messages and how to practice active listening._

   Example _(Student response.)_ _____

5. Dating can improve your negotiation skills. _(Sample answer:) Dating requires that young people consider others' opinions when decisions need to be made. This give-and-take process requires that each person be sensitive to the other's ideas and feelings._

   Example _(Student response.)_ _____

6. Dating can help you choose a marriage partner. _(Sample answer:) The dating process helps you learn about others and determine what is important to you in a marriage partner. Evaluating a dating relationship can help you decide if you should continue to develop the relationship and progress toward marriage._

   Example _(Student response.)_ _____

Beginning and Ending Relationships

Activity B

Name _____

Section 7:1

Date _____ Period _____

The desire to build dating relationships is part of the human need to feel accepted by others. Dating can help you grow and mature. Sometimes, however, your feelings about a relationship may change and the relationship may end. Learning to begin and end relationships can help you grow as a person.

For each of the words below, describe qualities that can help you begin a pair relationship.

1. Appearance: (Sample answer:) Good grooming, such as bathing regularly, maintaining an attractive hairstyle, and taking time to choose your clothing can help you make a positive impression on potential dating partners.

2. Attitude: (Sample answer:) Having a positive attitude and being friendly, confident, and courteous will demonstrate that you respect yourself and others. These traits will also make others want to get to know you.

3. Communication: (Sample answer:) Taking the first step by starting a conversation and asking open-ended questions can help you get to know potential dating partners. Active listening and eye contact can help you maintain communication.

4. Activities: (Sample answer:) Finding out what common interests you share with a dating partner can help you decide what activities to do together. As you spend time participating in shared activities, your friendship may grow.

When pair relationships end, the adjustment is easier if you focus on growing through the experience. Describe how each action below can help you grow through the pain of ending a relationship.

5. Be assertive, yet sensitive. (Sample answer:) If you are breaking off the relationship, be sensitive to the other's feelings. Explain why you feel the relationship needs to end.

6. Change dating patterns. (Sample answer:) It can be difficult to keep seeing your partner after you break up. Exploring new activities and interests can help you adjust.

7. Recognize that your feelings are normal. (Sample answer:) It is normal to experience feelings of pain and loneliness after a relationship ends. These feelings show that the relationship meant a lot to you, but it does not mean that breaking up was a mistake.

8. Emphasize other aspects of your life. (Sample answer:) Spending time with friends and family and pursuing new interests and hobbies can help you adjust. Focusing on other aspects of your life will also offer the opportunity to meet new people and eventually build other relationships.

Is It Love?

Activity C

Name _____

Section 7:2

Date _____ **Period** _____

Below are some questions to consider if you think you're in love. For each question, check the appropriate response. Answer the last question in the space provided.

(Answers are student response.)

	Yes	No
1. When you are together, do you feel comfortable and at ease? Can you be yourself without strain?	_____	_____
2. Has this relationship brought out the best in you? Are you more inclined to live up to your abilities?	_____	_____
3. When feelings of love are not present, is there still a continuing and stable bond between you?	_____	_____
4. Do you care a great deal about what happens to this person?	_____	_____
5. If this person became chronically ill and was always sick or was injured in an accident, would your feelings for him/her change?	_____	_____
6. Is this person physically attractive to you?	_____	_____
7. Do you feel proud to be seen together?	_____	_____
8. Do you agree on the items in life worth sacrificing for?	_____	_____
9. Have you known each other long enough to discover areas of disagreement?	_____	_____
10. Can you discuss topics that you disagree about and reach a mutual understanding?	_____	_____
11. When you disagree, does one person always feel unaccepted, wrong, or misunderstood?	_____	_____
12. Do you respect this person's mental abilities?	_____	_____
13. Can you accept his/her judgment?	_____	_____
14. Can and do you confide freely in this person, without any fear that what you share will be misjudged, criticized, or passed around?	_____	_____
15. Are you happy with this person's expression of affection for you?	_____	_____
16. Do you feel that both of you are committed to making this relationship succeed?	_____	_____

17. Based on your responses, do you feel that you have experienced romantic love or mature love? Explain. **(Student response.)** _____

_____

_____

_____

_____

The Benefits of Waiting Until Marriage

Activity D

Section 7:2

Name _____

Date _____ Period _____

When physical expressions of love are used early in a relationship, pressures to become sexually involved increase. Think about the psychological and physical consequences of premarital sexual activities. Then respond to the following questions.

1. How is true sexual freedom only possible within the commitment of marriage and mature love? **Sexual activity within marriage strengthens feelings of trust and openness. Waiting until marriage decreases the chances of anxiety about becoming pregnant, being rejected, getting a sexually transmitted infection, feeling guilty, experiencing reduced self-esteem, and possible misuse and abuse.**

2. What are some fears that sexual activity outside of marriage may cause? **fear of pregnancy, rejection, STIs, an ended relationship, and being used for the moment**

3. How could the functions of the brain and memory potentially affect future relationships? **The brain stores in memory past experiences and feelings of those experiences. Many early experiences are not positive due to lack of communication, openness, caring, and true concern, so many negative feelings about sex remain stored in the brain. These can impact future relationships.**

4. How could waiting until marriage strengthen a relationship? **Waiting builds trust. (A trusted person who has self-control before marriage will likely exercise self-control after marriage.) Waiting eliminates the possibility of developing negative feelings as a result of sexual experiences too early. Waiting helps a couple focus on building the intellectual, social, and emotional aspects of a relationship and safeguards a couple's health and ability to have children.**

(Continued)

Copyright by Goodheart-Willcox Co., Inc.

5. How could a pregnancy affect a teen's life? (Consider males and females.) less time to spend with friends, more time spent caring for a baby, difficulty in finishing school, difficultly in earning money to pay for child need's, less money for oneself and having fun, increased emotional strain from increased responsibilities

6. List three health risks for pregnant teens and their babies. anemia, or iron deficiency; low-birthweight babies; premature birth of child

Match the following descriptions of STIs with the appropriate terms.

___F___ 7. One of the most common bacterial STIs that can cause sterility if left untreated.

___A___ 8. A virus attacks the cells that normally help a person fight off infection and disease.

___C___ 9. An STI caused by a virus that infects the skin and mucous membranes and may cause genital warts.

___G___ 10. An STI caused by a virus that attacks the liver and can be spread by sexual contact or exposure to infected blood.

___D___ 11. An STI caused by a virus that produces a sore called a chancre.

___E___ 12. An STI resulting from an infection that grows in the warm, moist areas of the reproductive tract and in the eyes, mouth, or throat.

___B___ 13. An STI caused by a virus that results in repeated outbreaks of blisters.

___H___ 14. An STI that causes small bumps or clusters of bumps in the genital area.

___D___ 15. A rash, fever, sore throat, and headache are common symptoms of this STI.

___A___ 16. Fatigue, swollen lymph glands, dry cough, shortness of breath, fever, diarrhea, and rapid weight loss are symptoms of this STI.

A. AIDS
B. genital herpes
C. HPV
D. syphilis
E. gonorrhea
F. chlamydia
G. hepatitis
H. genital warts

Dating

Activity E Name ______________________

Section 7:2 Date ____________ Period ____________

1 MARRIAGE
2 ROMANTIC
3 PERSONAL
4 STEADY
5 ANEMIA
6 CHLAMYDIA
7 DEFICIENCY
8 HERPES
9 INFATUATION
10 HPV
11 ABSTINENCE
12 INTRAVENOUS
13 COURTEOUS
14 DATE RAPE
15 DOUBLE DATE
16 VIRUS
17 NEGOTIATE
18 GONORRHEA
19 COMMUNICATION
20 RESPONSIBLE
21 RAPE
22 SYPHILIS
23 SEXUALLY
24 PAIR
25 EVALUATE
26 COMPANIONSHIP
27 MATURE
28 GROOMING
29 GROUP

(Continued)

Read the descriptions and decide which chapter terms are being described. Write the correct terms in the crossword puzzle.

Across

1. Dating can help you choose a _____ partner.

3. _____ boundaries are limits for behavior that a person accepts in a relationship.

5. Pregnant teens may experience complications such as _____, or iron deficiency.

6. One of the most common bacterial STIs that can cause sterility if left untreated.

10. An STI that can lead to cervical cancer.

11. Not taking part in sexual activity is called _____.

13. _____ manners show that you respect and value others as people.

15. When two couples go out together, they _____.

17. Couples can learn to _____ when they make decisions together.

20. Being on time for a date shows that you are _____ and carry out your commitments.

21. Forced sexual intercourse is called _____.

22. An STI caused by bacteria that can be treated with an antibiotic such as penicillin.

24. In _____ dating, two people develop a relationship by spending time together as a couple.

26. Dating provides _____ for people who don't want to be alone.

27. _____ love is a long-lasting, caring, and giving type of love.

28. Personal appearance and good _____ are important in attracting a date.

Down

2. _____ love describes an exhilarating feeling toward a loved one.

4. When two people only date each other, they are _____ dating.

7. Acquired immune _____ syndrome weakens the body's immune system until it can no longer fight disease.

8. An STI caused by a virus, producing painful sores on the body.

9. Strong feeling of attraction that often is one-sided.

12. The _____ use of drugs can spread AIDS.

14. Sexual intercourse with a dating partner against one person's will is called _____.

16. AIDS is caused by the human immunodeficiency _____.

18. An STI that grows in the warm, moist areas of the reproductive tract and can be treated with an antibiotic.

19. Dating can improve _____ skills as couples talk and listen to each other.

23. STIs are _____ transmitted diseases.

25. You should _____ a relationship to determine whether or not to continue dating.

29. A date in which a group of people spend time together.

Chapter 8

Choosing to Marry

Maturing as a Person

Activity A   Name _____

Section 8:1   Date _____ Period _____

In the space provided, identify some of the qualities that are evidence of personal growth to maturity.

Quality	Describe how this quality affects a relationship	Example
Able to give love	Give of yourself to meet other's needs. Do what is best for other person. Builds love, rapport, appreciation; meets each other's needs.	Take time to share. Show love by actions. Express love in words.
Able to receive love	Your needs are met. You depend on each other.	Allow the other person to meet your needs.
Able to express empathy	Keeps relationship close. Know how to met each other's needs. Increases sharing. Increases attachment to each other. Helps mature love grow.	Thinking and feeling what the other person is feeling. Identify with each other. Sensitive to each other. Sharing deep and personal thought and feelings.
Emotionally stable	You can control your emotional responses. Increases good communication. Increase problem solving. Increase negotiation.	Use I-statements rather than name-calling. Take time to walk away and cool down when you become angry. Avoid name-calling, fighting.
Flexible	Allows give-and-take. Allows conflicts to be resolved. Consider needs and desires of all involved.	Willing to change. Considers other's views.
Decision-making skills	Couple can make decisions that will help them reach their goals. Increase satisfaction with life.	Makes decisions together. Set goal to finish college and reach it.
Age at marriage	Older person is more likely to be emotionally, socially, and mentally mature. Will likely have set goals and made plans to reach them.	Completed education, established in a job, financially independent, able to live on his or her own.

Inventory of Personal Readiness for Marriage

Activity B

Name_____

Section 8:2

Date _____ **Period** _____

The following activity will help you evaluate your readiness for marriage. Read each question.
Then place a check in the column that best represents how you feel about the question.

(Answers are student response.)

	Somtimes	Usually	Always
1. Am I able to unselfishly give love?	_____	_____	_____
2. Am I able to receive love?	_____	_____	_____
3. Am I sensitive to the hurts and needs of others?	_____	_____	_____
4. Am I willing to try, see, and experience the world from the other person's point of view?	_____	_____	_____
5. Can I recognize my own emotions?	_____	_____	_____
6. Can I accept my emotions and control them?	_____	_____	_____
7. Can I express my emotions without tearing down another person?	_____	_____	_____
8. Am I able and willing to adjust to change?	_____	_____	_____
9. Can I accept differences in a partner?	_____	_____	_____
10. Can I use give-and-take to resolve differences?	_____	_____	_____
11. Do I usually respond logically?	_____	_____	_____
12. Am I able to define issues?	_____	_____	_____
13. Do I think through the alternatives when making a decision?	_____	_____	_____
14. Am I responsible when evaluating alternatives?	_____	_____	_____

Similarities and Differences

Activity C   Name _____

Section 8:2   Date _____   Period _____

Working with your engagement simulation partner, discuss each of the following areas and identify similarities and differences. Answer the questions that follow as you relate them to potential marital quality. **(Answers are student response.)**

Interests

What do you like to do?

How would a lot of differences in interests affect a couple's ability to develop a high-quality marriage?

What interests would you be willing to develop in order to have something to do with your spouse that you both would enjoy?

What activities do you really dislike doing; that you would not consider as optional areas of interest you would be willing to develop?

Similarities: _____

_____

_____

Differences: _____

_____

_____

Values

What is important to you in life? (Consider personal areas, relationship areas, and work areas.)

What difficulties could arise in a relationship if a couple value different things in their lives? Give some examples.

Similarities: _____

_____

_____

Differences: _____

_____

_____

(Continued)

Goals

What do you want to do in life? (Consider personal, relationship, and work areas.)

What problems could arise for a couple if the individuals have very different goals in life?

Similarities: _____

_____

_____

Differences: _____

_____

_____

Backgrounds

Do you share similar backgrounds?

What are the benefits of having similar backgrounds as a couple?

What specific challenges could a couple experience if their backgrounds are very different?

Similarities: _____

_____

_____

Differences: _____

_____

_____

Final question: Are any of the above areas more important than others for building quality in your marital relationship? Explain. _____

_____

_____

_____

_____

How Do We Communicate?

Activity D

Name_____

Section 8:2

Date _____ Period _____

The following activity will help you evaluate your communication skills in preparation for marriage. Have a discussion about a relevant topic with your engagement simulation partner. Then read each statement. Place a check in the column that best represents how you feel about the statement.

(Answers are student response.)

	Usually	Sometimes	Rarely
1. We freely share personal thoughts and feelings.	____	____	____
2. We accept each other's points of view.	____	____	____
3. We listen actively, making sure we understand what is shared.	____	____	____
4. We do not spread what we have shared confidentially with each other.	____	____	____
5. Our communication helps us know each other intimately.	____	____	____
6. We communicate clearly, with few misunderstandings.	____	____	____

7. Explain how the above characteristics increase the quality of a marriage relationship. **When a couple communicate clearly, use active listening, and share personal thoughts and feelings, both people feel accepted and valued. When a couple trust each other, they can communicate openly. Good communication skills can also help a couple clear up misunderstandings, make joint decisions, and solve problems in a marriage.**

8. Explain how the following poor communication skills could affect the quality of a marriage relationship.

   A. Your partner always takes the opposite side of view. **(Sample answer:) You feel intimidated by your partner and stop expressing your opinions.**

   B. Your partner insists "I am right and you are wrong." **(Sample answer:) You feel that your partner does not value your opinion.**

   C. Your partner uses the silent treatment. **(Sample answer:) You feel hurt and ignored.**

   D. Your partner shares your innermost secrets with friends at a party. **(Sample answer:) You feel violated and no longer trust your partner. You stop communicating openly.**

   E. Your partner gives you advice most of the time. **(Sample answer:) You feel like your partner does not accept you as you are and does not respect your judgment.**

Evaluate Your Decision-Making and Problem-Solving Skills

Activity E

Name _____

Section 8:2

Date _____ **Period** _____

The following activity will help you evaluate your decision-making and problem-solving skills in preparation for marriage. With your engagement simulation partner, discuss a common problem that married couples might face and agree on a solution. Then read each statement. Place a check in the column that best represents how you feel about the statement.

(Answers are student response.)

	Usually True	Sometimes True	Rarely True
1. We disagree about little things.	_____	_____	_____
2. We both like to make our own decisions.	_____	_____	_____
3. We make decisions on impulse.	_____	_____	_____
4. We go by our gut-level feelings when we make decisions.	_____	_____	_____
5. We both want to prove our points when we disagree.	_____	_____	_____
6. Each expects the other to keep quiet when one disagrees with personal matters.	_____	_____	_____
7. We use comments such as "You should…" when we disagree.	_____	_____	_____
8. Each gets angry when not getting his or her own way.	_____	_____	_____
9. We yell and call each other names when upset.	_____	_____	_____
10. We try to figure out who's at fault to take the blame for a problem.	_____	_____	_____

11. Explain how the above characteristics impact the quality of a marriage relationship. **Poor decision-making and problem-solving skills can decrease the quality of a marriage. When partners do not make decisions jointly, they are not able to reach the goals they have set for their marriage. The relationship will suffer if problem-solving skills are not used to resolve disagreements.**

12. Describe decision-making skills that would add to the quality of a marriage relationship. **identify the issue; discuss different alternatives before making a decision; choose an alternative that satisfies both partners; develop a plan to carry out the decision; evaluate the decision together**

Our Expectations for Marriage

Activity F

Name_____

Section 8:3

Date _____ Period _____

As a couple plans marriage, the two need to discuss and reach an agreement on several areas. Discuss the following areas with your engagement simulation partner and record your opinions and desires. Mutually agree on the answers for each question, if you can. Note areas in which you strongly agree as well as strongly disagree.   **(Answers are student response.)**

Career goals and expectations

1. What are your career goals? _____

_____

2. Do you both plan to work? _____

3. What education do you want to get after high school? _____

4. How will you obtain it? _____

5. What are your values in the area of work? _____

_____

_____

Household arrangements

6. Where do you want to live? _____

7. Would you move if either spouse had an opportunity to advance in his or her career? _____

8. How will you manage household tasks? _____

_____

_____

Financial matters

9. Will you hold all assets jointly? _____

10. Will either person keep money, land, or assets held before marriage in his or her own name?

_____

11. How will income be managed? _____

_____

12. Whose income will pay what bills? _____

_____

13. How much spending money should each spouse have? _____

_____

(Continued)

Children

14. Do you want to have children? _____

15. How many? _____

16. When? _____

17. Will you try to adopt if you cannot have children? _____

18. How will child care and parenting responsibilities be handled? _____

_____

_____

Relationships with others

19. How much time will you spend with each other's family? _____

20. How will you spend holidays and traditional days of celebration? _____

21. How much time will you spend together with personal friends? _____

_____

22. How much time will you spend apart with your own personal friends? _____

_____

Your personal relationship

23. What expectations do you have for each other? _____

_____

_____

_____

Summary

24. How important do you think it will be for your future spouse to agree with you on questions such as these? _____

_____

_____

_____

_____

25. Are any of these areas so important that disagreement about them could cause a relationship to break apart? Describe and explain. _____

_____

_____

_____

Chapter 9

Adjusting to Marriage
Patterns of Adjustment

Activity A   **Name**_____

Section 9:1   **Date** _____   **Period** _____

A couple may try to adjust to differences in their relationship in different ways. In the following case, couples use one of these methods to try and settle their differences: hostility, concession, accommodation, or compromise. In each scenario, identify the pattern of adjustment they use. Next, judge how you think this pattern would affect the quality of the relationship. Finally, identify a method of adjustment that could result in a higher quality relationship.

Case 1

Andrea has to work late to complete a bid for a prospective job. She calls Matt to let him know she can't pick up their son at the babysitter, as previously planned. Matt gets upset because he is on his way to play basketball at the gym and does not want to change his plans. He yells at Andrea for not getting her work done on time, and complains that she is not sticking to her agreement to pick up their son. Andrea becomes angry and calls Matt inconsiderate and uncooperative.

Pattern of adjustment used: _hostility_____

Describe the effect it may have on the quality of their marriage relationship. _Hostility may deter open and intimate sharing, destroy feelings of love, tear down rapport between the couple, and thus weaken a relationship._

_____

_____

_____

_____

How do you think the disagreement could have been handled to give a more satisfactory solution to the problem? Explain your answer. _(Student response.)_____

_____

_____

_____

_____

_____

_____

_____

(Continued)

Case 2

Josea and Marcia did not believe their different religious backgrounds would affect their marriage relationship. One week they would attend a religious service that Josea preferred. The next week they would attend a religious service that Marcia preferred.

Pattern of adjustment used: accommodation _____

Describe the effect it may have on the quality of their marriage relationship. Accommodation does not increase the quality of the relationship, but it helps couples work around their differences.

_____

_____

Do you think a satisfactory solution was reached? Explain your answer. (Student response.) _____

_____

_____

_____

Case 3

For Josea and Marcia, the above arrangement worked well until they had children. Then, both parents wanted to raise the children in their own faith. This resulted in frequent disagreements until Josea finally agreed to let the children attend religious services with Marcia. He, however, did not join them and attended his church alone.

Pattern of adjustment used: concession and accommodation _____

Describe the effect it had on the quality of the marriage relationship and on the family. The arguments ended, but this decision did not strengthen the family. Instead of uniting the family, parents decided to go in different directions.

_____

_____

How do you think a more satisfactory solution could have been reached? Explain your answer. A more satisfactory solution would have been to agree on a service for all to attend together. This could have been accomplished through concession (one giving in to keep the family together) or compromise (in which they chose a new place of worship to attend as a family).

_____

_____

_____

_____

Becoming a Pair

Activity B   Name _____

Section 9:2   Date _____   Period _____

In the space provided, respond to the questions about interpersonal adjustments in marriage relationships.

1. Define the term *interpersonal adjustments*: Interpersonal adjustments include the changes a couple make as they learn to live with each other.

Pair Adjustments

2. Explain what it means to think of *we* instead of *me*. Give an example. Thinking of *we* instead of *me* requires recognizing your position as a member of a pair and considering the effect of actions on your partner. (Example is student response.)

Habits

3. Which of your habits may irritate a spouse? (Student response.)

4. How would you want another person to address you about an irritating habit? (Student response.)

Positive Feedback

5. Give four examples of ways you could show appreciation to a special friend (or spouse). (Student response.)

Communicating

6. At what time of day do you prefer to sit and talk? (Student response.)

7. If someone wanted you to change, what would be the best approach they could use? (Student response.)

(Continued)

8. What is the sandwich approach? putting a negative comment between two positive comments

_____

_____

9. How do you feel about using the sandwich approach? (Student response.)

_____

_____

Resolving Conflicts

10. Why is it necessary to identify the underlying source (the root problem) of an argument? because underlying issues will resurface in new arguments

_____

_____

11. Explain what you think is meant by the statement "When a married couple settle an argument, no one person wins and no one person loses." When an argument is settled or resolved, both win because the relationship is strengthened. If the argument is not resolved, both lose because the relationship is hurt by it.

_____

12. Why should old conflicts that are resolved be left in the past? Old conflicts brought up repeatedly serve as ammunition for new arguments. Attention should be focused on resolving the issues at hand.

_____

Active Interaction

13. What activities could you do with a spouse that would promote active interaction? (Student response.)

_____

_____

Emotional Needs

14. What emotional needs would you expect to have met in a marriage? (Student response.)

_____

_____

(Continued)

15. What other ways or outlets do you have for meeting some of your emotional needs (for example, hobbies)? (Student response.) _____

_____

_____

_____

16. List six elements of a relationship that can promote sexual satisfaction in a marriage. (List six:) _____
emotional bonding, love, trust, commitment, mutual respect, appreciation for each other,
sensitivity to each other's thoughts and desires

_____

Balance in the Relationship

17. How would you feel if your spouse was always in competition with you (for example, always wanting to make the final decision or take charge)? (Student response.) _____

_____

_____

18. How could you handle a situation in which your partner is competitive rather than cooperative? (Student response. Answers could include ideas such as open sharing, honest confrontation, showing acceptance of and respect for each other, and encouraging each other to reach personal goals and grow as persons.)

Adjusting to New Roles

19. List the roles you expect to have in marriage. (Student response.) _____

_____

_____

Role Expectations in Marriage

Name_____

Date _____ Period _____

When couples are able to live up to their role expectations of each other, their relationship is affected positively. In the space provided, identify your role expectations for yourself and your potential spouse. For example, what part do you expect to take in caring for the home? What part do you expect your spouse to carry out?

Realize that the expectations you have right now can change; they do not need to be set in concrete. Just identifying your expectations now can help you determine if these are valid long-term expectations. If they are, discussing these areas with a potential marriage partner will be important.

(Answers are student response.)

Home Maintenance Roles (caring for the home)	
Yourself	Spouse

Work Roles (holding a job, earning income)	
Yourself	Spouse

Money Management Roles (paying bills, making investments)	
Yourself	Spouse

Social Roles (socializing with friends, entertaining)	
Yourself	Spouse

Child Care Roles	
Yourself	Spouse

Chapter 10

Choosing to Parent

The Decision to Parent

Activity A

Name _____

Section 10:1

Date _____ **Period** _____

For this activity, pretend you are married. You and your spouse are trying to decide when to have children. Use the decision-making process below to think through this important decision.

1. Identify an issue that would require you to make a decision regarding when to have children.
   (Student response.) _____

2. List the alternatives you have (for example, when you finish your education or have a good job).
   (Student response.) _____

   _____
   _____
   _____
   _____
   _____

3. Consider the alternatives. Think about the advantages and disadvantages of each alternative, as well as the possible effects on your life. Refer to Figure 10-1 in the text for some questions to consider.
   (Chart answers are student response.)

Alternatives	Advantages	Disadvantages	Effects on Your Lives
A. Have children now, during the teen years			
B. Have children in two years			

(Continued)

Alternatives	Advantages	Disadvantages	Effects on Your Lives
C. Have children when 22 to 25 years old			
D. Have children when age 30 or older			

4. Choose which alternative you feel would be the best for you and your spouse. Explain why you made this choice. (Student response.) _____

_____

_____

_____

_____

_____

_____

5. List four healthy reasons for wanting to parent and choosing parenthood. (List four: a way to pass part of yourself into the future; share your life with a new, younger life; extend the family into a new generation; have the personal experience of having children; share love and guide a child to adulthood; the rewarding experience of parenthood)

_____

6. List four unhealthy reasons people might give for wanting to become parents. (List four: prestige, pressure from family or friends, show physical competence, gain personal power over the child or partner, gain love from the child, improve their marriage)

_____

_____

Parent Opinion Survey

Activity B

Name _____

Section 10:2

Date _____ **Period** _____

Conduct a three-part interview with a parent to find out his or her opinions about parenting. For Part One, fill in the background information about the parent in the space provided. Then ask the parent the survey questions that follow in Part Two. Place a check in the column that best represents the parent's opinion. For Part Three, write in the parent's responses to the questions. After finishing these three parts, read the directions for completing this activity on the next page.

Part One: Background Information (Student response.)

1. The parent you interviewed: _____
   A. mother
   B. father

2. The parent's age: _____

3. The parent's occupation: _____

4. Number of children: _____

5. Ages of children: _____

6. Parent's age when first child was born: _____

Part Two: Parent Opinion Survey (Student response.)

	Strongly Agree	Agree	Disagree	Strongly Disagree
1. I was well-prepared to be a parent.				
2. I planned the conception and birth of my child/children.				
3. Parenting is harder than I thought it would be.				
4. Becoming a parent is the best way for a person to develop into a mature and responsible adult.				
5. Childrearing is fun.				
6. If I had known what parenthood involved, I might not have had children.				
7. Children improve a marriage.				
8. People are poorly prepared for parenthood.				
9. Children will turn out well if they have good parents.				
10. Parents often expect their children to succeed in areas in which they failed.				
11. Having and raising children costs more than I expected.				
12. If I could go back in time, I would have fewer or no children.				
13. If I could, I would have more children.				

(Continued)

Part Three: Short-Answer Questions   (Student response.)

1. What do you wish you had known before having children? _____

_____

_____

_____

2. What have you liked best about being a parent? _____

_____

_____

_____

3. What has been the most difficult part of being a parent? _____

_____

_____

_____

After completing the survey, write a report summarizing the interview:

A. Describe the parent who responded to the interview using the background information you obtained.

B. Give your personal views of the parent's responses to the survey.

C. Describe how your personal attitudes and expectations about parenting are similar to or different from those of the parent you interviewed. (Student response.) _____

_____

_____

_____

_____

_____

_____

_____

_____

_____

_____

_____

_____

_____

Myth or Reality?

Activity C

Name _____

Section 10:3

Date _____ Period _____

Read each of the following statements about the myths and realities of parenting. Circle *F* if you think the statement is false or expresses a myth. Circle *T* if you think the statement is true or expresses the realities of parenting.   **(Student response.)**

T   F   1. I see my child as a robust and healthy baby.

T   F   2. I think my child will look like me.

T   F   3. My child will be athletic and bright.

T   F   4. Children will complicate our life.

T   F   5. The joys of children certainly will outweigh any difficulties.

T   F   6. Parenting responsibilities don't need to interfere with my career.

T   F   7. I believe my mate would be less likely to leave me if we had a child.

T   F   8. We will evenly split child care responsibilities between us.

T   F   9. We can get by on one income as well as two if we are careful with our spending.

T   F   10. We will be able to go out as much as we did before the baby arrives. We'll just take the baby with us.

T   F   11. We can spend as much time with friends as always. We'll just have them come to our house.

T   F   12. Food expenses won't increase because breast-feeding will take care of all the baby's food needs.

T   F   13. Our health insurance will automatically cover the baby when he or she is born.

T   F   14. High quality in-home child care is easy to find.

T   F   15. When our children are grown, we will spend holidays together.

T   F   16. Parenthood is mostly fun.

T   F   17. Parenthood is the most personally rewarding step a person can take in life.

T   F   18. Children can help parents avoid being lonely in later life.

T   F   19. Parenthood brings out the best in a person.

T   F   20. If we wait until we have enough money, we will never have children.

Think about the statements you marked *false*. If a person believed these statements to be reality, what problems might arise after the person becomes a parent? **(Student response.)** _____

_____

_____

_____

_____

_____

Preparing for Children

Activity D   Name _____

Section 10:3   Date _____ Period _____

Answer the following questions involving parenting decisions.

1. Describe how a child impacts a family in each of the following ways.
   A. Time: less time to spend alone or as a couple

   _____

   B. Finances: increased expenses, yet couple may have decreased income if one parent
      takes time off to provide care for the child

   C. Lifestyle: needs to include time with the child

   _____

2. Describe the impact on a family if spouses want to have children but cannot. Some feel they
   have missed out on an important aspect of life and may be depressed, even desperate to
   have a child.

3. The two main causes of infertility in men include ___low sperm count___ and ___blocked tubes___.

4. The two main causes of infertility in women include hormonal factors and blocked fallopian tubes.

5. List three harmful factors that might contribute to infertility in both sexes. (List three:) exposure
   to radiation or toxic chemicals, smoking tobacco or marijuana, STIs

   _____

   _____

6. List and describe the most common reproductive technology procedure used to help families have
   children. In vitro fertilization is used to overcome blocked fallopian tubes. Multiple eggs
   are stimulated to mature. The mature eggs are removed from the ovaries and fertilized in
   the laboratory with the husband's sperm. After cell division has begun, the fertilized eggs
   are placed directly into the uterus.

7. What are some ethical and legal problems that may result from using various reproductive
   technologies to have children? (Sample answers:) tampering with the biological process;
   determining who can claim the right to the child if a donor sperm or egg is used

   _____

   _____

8. Describe the preparation process adoption agencies take to place children in appropriate homes.
   (See pages 220–221 in the text.)

   _____

   _____

Chapter 11

Pregnancy and Childbirth

Prenatal Development

Activity A Name _____

Section 11:1 Date _____ Period _____

Part One: Match the following definitions or functions with the appropriate terms. (Answers may be used more than once.)

__C__	1.	One sperm and one egg unite.
__D__	2.	The first two months of development.
__B__	3.	Surrounds and protects the baby until birth.
__H__	4.	Carries waste products away from the baby.
__G__	5.	The condition of carrying a developing child.
__F__	6.	An organ in which the mother's blood vessels meet with the baby's capillaries.
__A__	7.	Acts as a cushion for the fetus.
__H__	8.	Carries oxygen, nutrients, and antibodies to the growing baby.
__E__	9.	The last seven months of development.
__F__	10.	Prevents some harmful substances, such as bacteria, from reaching the baby.

A. amniotic fluid
B. amniotic sac
C. conception
D. embryo stage
E. fetal stage
F. placenta
G. pregnancy
H. umbilical cord

Part Two: Match the following stages of fetal development with the appropriate month. (Answers may be used more than once.)

__E__	1.	Pasty substance called vernix coats the fetus' skin.
__A__	2.	Zygote implants into uterine wall.
__F__	3.	Eyelids open and shut.
__B__	4.	Brain begins to coordinate the functions of the internal organs.
__I__	5.	Birth occurs.
__G__	6.	Baby has a 90 percent chance of surviving; brain can control hearing, sight, and smell.
__C__	7.	Kidney functions and produces urine.
__H__	8.	Limbs become smooth and plump.
__I__	9.	Lightening takes place.
__D__	10.	The mother usually first begins to notice fetus movement.

A. first month
B. second month
C. third month
D. fourth month
E. fifth month
F. sixth month
G. seventh month
H. eighth month
I. ninth month

Prenatal Care

Name_____

Date _____ Period _____

Proper prenatal care provides a healthy environment for the developing baby. In the space provided, complete the following questions about prenatal care.

1. What is a recommended schedule for prenatal visits to a health professional? _monthly for the first six months; twice a month during the seventh and eighth months; weekly during the ninth month_

2. Explain the functions of the following.
    A. obstetrician-gynecologist: _a specialist who provides medical and surgical care to women_
    B. family practitioner: _a medical doctor who provides health care for all family members_
    C. certified nurse-midwife: _a registered nurse who has training to provide health care for normal pregnancies and births_

3. Using www.mypyramid.gov, create a "MyPyramid Plan for Moms." Assume that the woman is pregnant, 25 years old, 5'7" tall, and 130 pounds. Also assume she does 30 to 60 minutes of physical activity daily, and that the baby is due eight months from today's date. For each food group below, list the recommended number of ounce-equivalents that the woman should eat in each trimester.

	First Trimester	Second Trimester	Third Trimester
Grains	7 ounces	9 ounces	9 ounces
Vegetables	3 cups	3½ cups	3½ cups
Fruits	2 cups	2 cups	2 cups
Milk	3 cups	3 cups	3 cups
Meat & Beans	6 ounces	6½ ounces	6½ ounces

4. What is an average recommended weight gain for a pregnant woman? _30 pounds_

5. How is the pregnant woman's total weight gain divided? List in order of amount.

Weight of baby	7½
Placenta	1½
Amniotic fluid	2
Increased size of uterus	2
Increased breast size	2
Extra blood	4
Extra fluid in body tissues	4
Extra fat stored in body	7

6. What are the two best and safest physical activities for a pregnant woman? _swimming, walking_

7. How many hours of sleep are recommended for a pregnant woman? _eight hours each night and a short rest during the day_

Prenatal Effects and the Unborn Child

Activity C

Name _____

Section 11:2

Date _____ **Period** _____

Match the definitions or descriptions about prenatal effects on the unborn child with the appropriate terms.

___E___ 1. A condition that exists from birth and limits the ability of a person's body or mind.

___A___ 2. A test that measures the amount of alphafetoprotein produced by the baby and passed to the mother's blood.

___K___ 3. Constricts the blood vessels in the mother and baby, often resulting in low birthweight.

___I___ 4. May cause mutations that result in birth defects.

___L___ 5. A birth defect in which the nerves are open along the spine.

___M___ 6. The birth of a dead fetus.

___D___ 7. The absence of all or a major part of the fetus' brain.

___F___ 8. A pattern of disability—identified by a small head, small eye openings, and mental retardation—due to alcoholism in the mother.

___H___ 9. A complication of pregnancy that causes high blood pressure, swelling, and protein in the urine.

___N___ 10. Use of sound waves that bounce off the fetus and project onto a monitor; used to monitor the development of the fetus.

___C___ 11. A procedure used to draw fluid from the uterus to examine cells cast off by the fetus.

___G___ 12. Death of a fetus born before the sixth month, too early to have developed enough for survival in the outside world.

___J___ 13. A type of measles that can cause miscarriage, stillbirth, or birth defects.

___B___ 14. Can cause problems in the development of the fetus' brain, eyes, heart, limbs, and joints.

A. AFP blood test
B. alcohol
C. amniocentesis
D. anencephaly
E. birth defect
F. fetal alcohol syndrome
G. miscarriage
H. preeclampsia
I. radiation
J. rubella
K. smoking
L. spina bifida
M. stillbirth
N. ultrasound

The Cost of Having a Baby

Activity D

Name_____

Section 11:3

Date _____ **Period** _____

Use a catalog or visit a department store to figure the approximate cost of preparing for a new baby's physical needs. Then inquire at a local clinic and hospital to determine the cost of prenatal care and hospital delivery. **(Student response.)**

Items	Cost	Items	Cost
Clothing		**Furniture and Linens**	
Four cotton knit nightgowns	_____	Crib (or bassinet)	_____
Four cotton knit undershirts	_____	Dresser	_____
Three sweaters	_____	Changing table	_____
One knit cap	_____	Two sets of crib sheets	_____
Three dozen disposable or cloth diapers	_____	Two blankets	_____
Three plastic pants	_____	Bumper pad set for crib	_____
Four pairs of socks	_____	Plastic tub for bathing	_____
Four bibs	_____	Diaper pail	_____
One outfit for special occasions	_____	Infant car seat	_____
Baby Care Supplies		**Prenatal and Delivery Costs**	
Baby soap	_____	Doctor's fee	_____
Cotton balls	_____	Average hospital fee	_____
Baby oil and lotion	_____		
Baby powder	_____		
Premoistened towelettes	_____		
Manicure scissors (made for babies)	_____		
Hairbrush and comb (made for babies)	_____		

The total cost of preparing for a baby's physical needs is $_____.

Pregnancy and Childbirth

Activity E

Section 11:4

Name _____

Date _____ Period _____

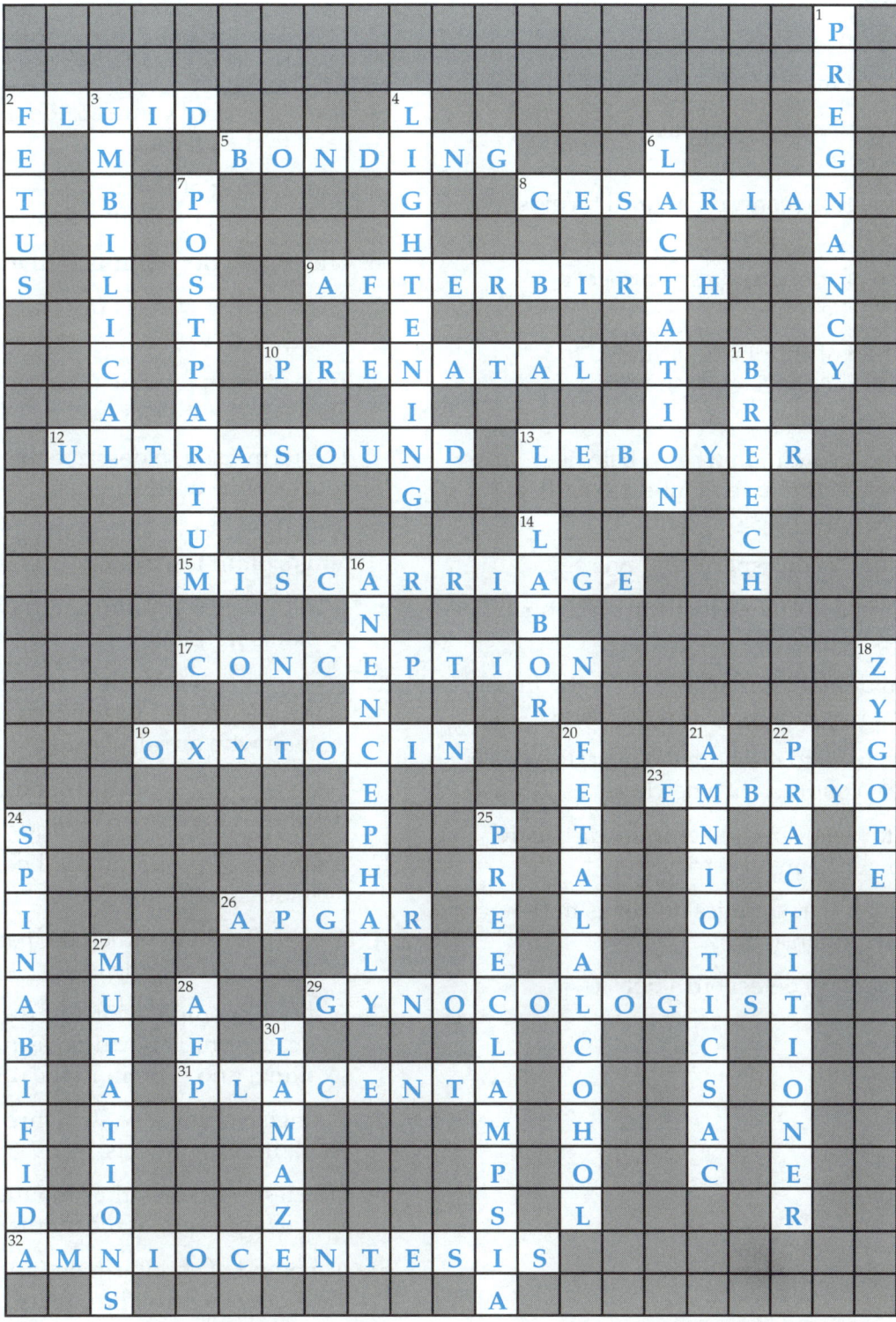

(Continued)

Read the descriptions and decide which chapter terms are being described. Write the correct terms in the crossword puzzle.

Across

2. The amniotic _____ acts as a cushion for the fetus.

5. An attachment between parents and child.

8. A surgical method of delivering a baby.

9. The placenta that is expelled after the baby is born.

10. The time from conception until birth is called the _____ period.

12. The use of sound waves to project an image of the fetus.

13. A method of childbirth designed to decrease the shock of birth for the newborn.

15. A medical condition when a baby is born before the sixth month, too early to survive in the outside world.

17. The union of one sperm and one egg.

19. A placental hormone that starts the birth process.

23. A term describing the growing baby in the first two months of development.

26. A scale used to measure the overall physical condition of a newborn.

29. A doctor who specializes in medical care for women is an obstetrician-_____.

31. The organ that supplies nutrients to the growing, unborn baby.

32. A test used to detect birth defects.

Down

1. The condition of carrying a developing child.

2. The growing baby during the last seven months of development.

3. The _____ cord connects the unborn baby to the placenta.

4. The shifting of the uterus downward and forward before the baby is born.

6. The production of milk in the breasts.

7. The first few weeks after childbirth is the _____ period.

11. Type of birth in which the baby is positioned buttocks first.

14. The term used to describe the contractions of the uterus.

16. A birth defect in which all or part of the fetus's brain is absent.

18. A cell with 46 chromosomes that implants in the uterus.

20. _____ _____ syndrome is a pattern of disabilities found in children born to women who are alcoholics.

21. The _____ _____ is a membrane that surrounds and protects the unborn baby.

22. A family _____ is a medical doctor who provides health care.

24. A birth defect in which the nerves are open along the spine is _____ _____.

25. A serious complication of pregnancy that causes high blood pressure, swelling, and protein in the urine.

27. Changes in the gene structure that can result in birth defects.

28. This test measures the amount of alphafetoprotein in the mother's blood.

30. A method of childbirth designed to help the mother control the pain of childbirth.

Chapter 12

Helping Children Grow and Develop

Support Our Future: Give Aid to Needy Children

Activity A   Name_____

Section 12:1   Date _____   Period _____

Read the scenario that follows. Then write a letter that states these programs should be funded as they are a good investment for society. Present at least three reasons to support your point of view. (You may wish to refer to www.mypyramid.gov as a source of information.) After finishing your letter, complete the evaluation form on the next page.

Scenario: The government is considering a bill to increase government funding of child nutrition programs.

(Letter is student response.)

_____

_____

_____

_____

_____

_____

_____

_____

_____

_____

_____

_____

_____

_____

_____

_____

_____

_____

_____

_____

(Continued)

First, complete a self-evaluation of your letter using the checklist below. Next, exchange letters with a classmate and answer the questions that follow.

Part One: Self-Evaluation

Reread your letter. Review it for the following points, placing a check in the appropriate column for each point. **(Student response.)**

	Yes	No
1. Have you stated your point of view?	_____	_____
2. Have you specified your purpose?	_____	_____
3. Have you identified a problem?	_____	_____
4. Have you presented facts and information to support your view?	_____	_____
5. Have you interpreted the facts to support your view?	_____	_____
6. Have you made any incorrect assumptions?	_____	_____
7. Have you identified a solution?	_____	_____
8. Have you identified the consequences of your solution?	_____	_____

Have you covered all the points? If so, you have done an excellent job of presenting a logical argument to support your point of view. Circle the rating that best represents your self-evaluation.

Excellent   Good   Fair   Poor

Part Two: Peer Evaluation

Answer the following questions regarding your classmate's letter.

1. What is the writer's point of view? **that the nutrition programs should be funded**

2. What is the writer's purpose? **to convince the reader to fund the nutrition programs**

3. What is the problem the writer has identified? **(Student response.)**

4. List the facts used to support the point of view. **(Student response.)**

5. What problems can you identify with the way the facts are interpreted? **(Student response.)**

6. What assumptions can you identify that the writer has made? **(Student response.)**

7. Does the writer present a logical solution? What is it? **(Student response.)**

8. What are the consequences that the writer has suggested for this solution? **(Student response.)**

Were you able to answer all of these questions? If so, the writer has done an excellent job of writing a letter to support his or her point of view. Circle the rating that best represents your evaluation.

Excellent   Good   Fair   Poor

Milestones of Development

Name _____

Date _____   Period _____

Identify ways that people in a child's environment can stimulate the child's development in each area.

Area of Development	Milestones of Development	Ways to Stimulate Development
Physical Development • Gross-motor behavior • Fine-motor behavior	Rolling over Sitting Crawling Walking Running Skipping Holding a pencil or crayon Scribbling Drawing Buttoning Cutting Tracing	(Sample answers:) Give child space to move around Provide toys for child to grasp, shake, squeeze Provide toys for gross-motor activities like riding toys Provide child opportunities to play with crayons, paint, paper Provide small toys for child to manipulate
Intellectual Development	Imprinting on brain Memory Symbols Language Crying Cooing Babbling Imitation of sounds Expressive jargon One-word sentences Concrete operations Abstract operations	(Sample answers:) Talk to child Sing to child Read books to child Label things in the environment Provide toys that promote creative play (building blocks, sorting toys) Play various games that develop thinking skills Assist children in learning

(Continued)

Area of Development	Milestones of Development	Ways to Stimulate Development
Social Development	Bonding with caregiver Developing peer relationships	(Sample answers:) Interact with young child, looking into their eyes, talking, smiling, caressing their skin Provide opportunities to interact with other caregivers Provide opportunities to play with other children Model desired behaviors
Emotional Development	Feelings of security Feelings of love Feelings of trust Feelings of competence or being capable	(Sample answers:) Parents need to meet child's needs for food, clothing, shelter Parents need to provide a secure and safe environment Parents need to hold, cuddle, and caress young children Parents need to provide opportunities for children to try things and be successful Children need opportunities to develop close friendships

Child Observation and Evaluation

Activity C   Name_____

Section 12:3   Date _____   Period _____

Choose one stage of a child's development. Observe the child's physical, social, intellectual, and emotional behaviors during this stage. Use the chart below to record your observations and your conclusions about the child's development. Then write a brief report, following the directions at the bottom of the page.   **(Student response.)**

Observation Record

Physical Development	
Activity:	Behavior Observed:
Conclusions about child's development:	

Social Development	
Activity:	Behavior Observed:
Conclusions about child's development:	

Intellectual Development	
Activity:	Behavior Observed:
Conclusions about child's development:	

Emotional Development	
Activity:	Behavior Observed:
Conclusions about child's development:	

On a separate sheet of paper, summarize your observations in a brief report that includes the following points:

1. A description of the child's physical, social, intellectual, and emotional development and the observations that support the evaluation.

2. A description of the actions and activities that parents and caregivers could use to stimulate this child's development.

Growth and Development Terms

Name_____

Date _____   Period _____

Read the definitions relating to children's growth and development. Then write the appropriate terms in the blanks.

__maturation__ 1. The emergence of physical characteristics through the growth process.

__pattern__ 2. Several events that take place in a certain order.

__rate of development__ 3. The speed at which a child proceeds through a developmental pattern. (three words)

__obesity__ 4. A condition marked by excess body fat.

__diseases__ 5. Some are prevented by giving children immunizations.

__nurturing__ 6. An environment in which a child feels loved and supported.

__role model__ 7. A person who models acceptable behavior for how people should live and act. (two words)

__temperament__ 8. Patterns for responding to the environment.

__milestones__ 9. Major accomplishments within each area of development.

__stranger anxiety__ 10. Experienced by an infant when someone unfamiliar comes near. (two words)

__gross-motor behavior__ 11. Movements that use the large muscles. (three words)

__cortisol__ 12. Under stress, this hormone washes over the developing brain, producing an acid-wash effect.

__intellectual development__ 13. The growth of mental skills. (two words)

__concrete__ 14. Thinking patterns in which children mentally review specific actions and experiences.

__social development__ 15. The process in which children learn to adapt to the world around them. (two words)

__bonding__ 16. A strong feeling of attachment.

__emotional development__ 17. A process in which children learn to identify their feelings and control the accompanying behavior. (two words)

__symbols__ 18. Thought-pictures of objects.

__separation anxiety__ 19. Experienced by an infant who moves too far from his or her mother. (two words)

__autonomy__ 20. The knowledge that a person is separate from others and has control over his or her body.

Chapter 13

Caring for and Guiding Children

Creating a Nurturing Environment

Activity A　　　　　　　　　　　　　　Name _____

Section 13:1　　　　　　　　　　　　　Date _____ Period _____

Read the text to discover how a parent can help a child feel secure, protected, accepted, and loved. Then answer the questions that follow.

1. List four ways that a parent can help a child feel loved. **(List four:) verbal messages; nonverbal messages such as tone of voice and amount of attention; making direct eye contact; providing close physical contact; spending time together**

_____

_____

_____

_____

2. In each of the following situations, suggest a parental response that will help the child feel loved.

   A. While pouring milk in her glass, five-year-old Ilsa spills some on the table. **(Sample answer:) reassure Ilsa that accidents happen and help her wipe up the milk**

   B. Three-year-old Michael is afraid to go to bed because of the thunder and lightning. **(Sample answer:) explain to Michael that the family's home provides shelter from the weather**

   C. Four-year-old Toby accidentally wets the bed during the night. **(Sample answer:) tell Toby that the accidents will stop as he gets older, but help him remember to go to the bathroom before bedtime**

   D. Fourteen-year-old Candy is upset because she did not make first-string on the basketball team. **(Sample answer:) remind Candy that she is loved, and that she will have other successes to celebrate**

   E. Josh and Eli are running around the room while their parents discuss an important decision that has to be made that evening. **(Sample answer:) stop the boys from running by getting them interested in some toys or a game**

Providing Guidance

Name _____

Date _____   Period _____

Match the following definitions with the appropriate guidance terms.

___B___ 1. Acting in a way that you want your children to act.

___H___ 2. Making sure children know what is and what is not acceptable behavior.

___D___ 3. Encouraging and praising desired behavior.

___A___ 4. Setting a pattern to follow every day and keep.

___F___ 5. Guiding a child from one activity to a more acceptable activity.

___G___ 6. Guiding children's actions by asking them to do something.

___C___ 7. Helping a child learn from his or her mistakes by not interfering with the results.

___E___ 8. Controlling children's behavior by giving them a reason to regret engaging in behavior they knew was wrong.

A. establishing routines
B. modeling
C. natural consequences
D. positive reinforcement
E. punishment
F. redirecting
G. requesting
H. setting limits

9. Why should punishment *not* be used on very young children? For punishment to be effective, the child needs to be old enough to understand wrong behavior. Parents should only use a punishment that fits the wrong behavior.

_____

_____

_____

_____

_____

10. Why should parents *not* use punishment when they are angry? The goal of punishment is *not* to give the parents a chance to vent their anger. Punishment dealt under these circumstances will likely tear down the child's self-esteem and may be abusive.

_____

_____

_____

_____

_____

Choosing a Method of Guidance

Activity C

Name_____

Section 13:2

Date _____ Period _____

For each scenario below, suggest the most effective method of guidance. Remember, whatever method of guidance is used, it should go hand-in-hand with a high level of support, love, and acceptance.

1. Eight-year-old Thomas is putting dishes away. He throws a spoon at his ten-year-old sister who is teasing him about completing his share of household tasks. How should this situation be handled? (Sample answer:) The parents can punish Thomas for engaging in wrong behavior by making him do his sister's tasks as well.

2. Two-year-old Lauren does not like to go to bed. Every night she crawls out of bed, asks for a drink of water, and asks to go to the bathroom. How would you suggest her parents handle this situation? (Sample answer:) Her parents can establish a routine of getting Lauren a drink and taking her to the bathroom every night before putting her to bed.

3. Nine-year-old Alicia hears her mother respond to the telephone caller, "No, he's not here right now." Alicia knows her dad is sleeping on the couch. Later, Alicia's mother asks her how she did on the history test she had that day. "It went great," she says. "I did fine." Her mother was surprised when Alicia's teacher sent a progress report later that week stating Alicia had failed the test. How should Alicia's mother handle this situation? (Sample answer:) Alicia's mother should model positive behavior instead of negative behavior.

4. Only three weeks after getting his license, sixteen-year-old Derek gets a speeding ticket while driving the family car. He does not have the money to pay the $69.00 fine. How should his parents respond to this situation? (Sample answer:) The parents can restrict Derek's driving privileges until he has saved up enough to pay them back for the fine.

5. Thirteen-year-old Tasha begs her parents to let her stay out with her friends until 1:00 in the morning. How should her parents respond? (Sample answer:) Tasha's parents can let her go and learn the natural consequences of staying up late by not allowing her to take a nap.

6. Alex's grandfather is mixing cement in a bucket to set a swing set pole. Two-year-old Alex reaches into the bucket and grabs a handful of cement. How should Alex's grandfather respond? (Sample answer:) Alex's grandfather should redirect Alex to play with some toys or another appropriate activity.

7. When she changes clothes, Amy drops them on the floor and leaves them. Her room is always a mess! Suggest a method of guidance that could help Amy get organized. (Sample answer:) Amy's parents could request that she pick up her things in a way that will not damage her self-esteem.

Choosing a Quality Toy

Activity D   **Name** _____

Section 13:3   **Date** _____ **Period** _____

Review the guidelines for toy selection in the text. Then choose a toy from a catalog or store that you feel has the qualities of a good toy. In the space below, attach a picture of the toy. Explain why you think this is a quality toy, giving reasons to support your point of view. Finally, develop an advertising slogan to promote this toy.

1. Attach a picture of the toy here.

    (Student response.)

2. Explain why you think this is a good quality toy. Give reasons to support your point of view.
    (Student response.)
    _____
    _____
    _____
    _____
    _____
    _____

3. Develop an advertising slogan that you think would promote this toy's high quality for children. Be sure to identify the age group for which you feel this toy is appropriate. (Student response.)
    _____
    _____
    _____

Age-Appropriate Toys

Activity E

Name _____

Section 13:3

Date _____ **Period** _____

Choose one stage of children's development. Develop a list of toys that matches the children's age and skill level. Then complete the chart below. (Include toys that promote growth and development in all four areas: physical, intellectual, social, and emotional.)

Choosing Toys for Children

Stage of development: (Student response.)	Age of children in this group: (Student response.)
Age-appropriate toys: (Student response.)	Type of play developed: (Student response.)

Tips for Parents

Name _____

Date _____ Period _____

1. For each area below, list tips for parents to help them guide their children in developing healthy living habits.

	To help children develop healthy habits, parents can:
Eating Habits	Choose the recommended amounts from each of the food groups. Serve nutritious snacks. Avoid serving foods with too much sugar, salt, and fats. Make food look appetizing by combining different colors, textures, and shapes. Involve children in food preparation. Encourage children to try new foods.
Sleeping Habits	Make sure that the young child has time for adequate sleep. Observe behavior to determine if the child is getting enough sleep.
Physical Activity Habits	Limit the time allowed for sedentary activities. Emphasize that physical activity includes any movement during the day, not just structured exercise or sports. Encourage active leisure activities such as participation in sports.
Dental Care Habits	Make sure children get plenty of milk and dairy products, use fluoridated toothpaste, brush regularly, and get regular checkups.
Medical Care Habits	Get regular checkups. Follow an immunization schedule. Keep children home when they have childhood diseases.

2. Identify a routine for each area that could help a parent meet the child's needs for health and safety. Be creative.

	Sample Routines That Could Meet a Child's Needs for Health and Safety
Eating Routine	(Student response.)
Sleeping Routine	(Student response.)
Physical Activity Routine	(Student response.)
Dental Routine	(Student response.)
Medical Care Routine	(Student response.)

Chapter 14

Today's Family

Changes in the American Family

Activity A Name_____

Section 14:1 Date _____ Period _____

American families have faced challenges and changes throughout history. Review the "Trends in American Family Life" section on pages 305–309 in the text. In the space provided, compare and contrast family life during the following eras: colonial, industrial revolution, and technological age.

The Colonial Family

1. Identify the type of work that fueled the economy during this era. Describe the relationship between the worker and other workers in society.
   The work centered around agriculture. Workers were self-sufficient.
   _____
   _____
   _____

2. Identify the roles of the mother. raised food, sewed garments, made candles and soap, cared for children, may have helped in the field

3. Identify the roles of the father. worked in the fields, hunted for food
   _____

4. Identify the roles of children in the family. helped parents, cared for younger siblings, worked in the fields

5. Describe the roles of extended family members. interacted socially, helped with daily living needs, worked together to meet the needs of the family

The Family in the Industrial Revolution

6. Identify the type of work that fueled the economy during this era. Describe the relationship between the worker and other workers in the society.
   factory work; dependent on others
   _____
   _____
   _____

(Continued)

7. Identify the roles of the mother. _stayed home, raised children, did housework_____

_____

8. Identify the roles of the father. _worked at a job that required spending long hours away from home_____

9. Identify the roles of children in the family. _helped around home, went to work as soon as they were old enough to get a job_____

10. Describe the roles of extended family members. _were often far away, provided less support for family_____

The Family in the Technological Age

11. Identify the type of work that fuels the economy during this era. Describe the relationship between the worker and other workers in the society. _work requiring greater skills, a service- and information-oriented society_____

_____

_____

12. Identify the roles of the mother. _may work outside the home, still main caregiver for children, companion to husband_____

13. Identify the roles of the father. _works outside the home, often shares parenting and household management tasks, companion to wife_____

14. Identify the roles of children in the family. _may have more responsibilities sharing household management tasks, more emphasis on education and gaining skills_____

15. Describe the roles of extended family members. _usually live far away, but make contact via e-mail, telephone, air travel, and other tools of technology_____

The Changing Family

16. In what ways has family living changed for the better over time? _(Student response.)_____

_____

17. In what ways has family living become more difficult? _(Student response.)_____

_____

18. What can people learn from families in the past to help prepare for possible future changes? _Throughout history, the family has adjusted to various challenges and survived. It continues to be a strong and important unit of society._____

How Does the Family Carry Out Its Functions?

Activity B

Name _____

Section 14:2

Date _____ **Period** _____

Match the following family activities with the functions of the family that are being carried out by the activity. (Some may have more than one right answer.) Be prepared to explain your choice.

B, C 1. Reading a story to a child before he or she goes to bed.

A 2. Making family meals.

C, D 3. Having a child help clean the house.

A 4. Working to make money to pay family living expenses.

A, C 5. Playing touch football.

C 6. Attending a house of worship.

B 7. Listening to a child, giving full attention and direct eye contact.

C, D 8. Having a child help set the table.

D 9. Providing music lessons for your child.

A 10. Taking a sick child to the doctor.

D 11. Encouraging your child to take an advanced math class.

B 12. Giving a child a hug.

A 13. Buying clothing for your child.

B 14. Attending a child's sporting events.

D 15. Saving money for a child's college education.

A, C 16. Taking a toddler to play in the park.

D 17. Helping a child with homework.

B, D 18. Encouraging a child to believe he or she can succeed.

C 19. Redirecting a child to an appropriate activity.

C 20. Enforcing a natural consequence as a means of guiding behavior.

A. meeting physical needs
B. meeting emotional needs
C. socializing children
D. influencing roles in society

21. Explain how some of the above activities could fulfill more than one function of the family.
(Sample answer:) Some activities, such as taking a toddler to play in the park, not only fulfill physical needs for exercise but also provide opportunities to socialize with other children. Reading a story could socialize a child by spending time with him or her and also meet emotional needs.

Family Structures

Activity C

Name_____

Section 14:3

Date _____ **Period** _____

Match the various characteristics with the types of family structures they describe. Answers may be used more than once.

___B___ 1. Has only one parent to fulfill many responsibilities and roles of parenting.

___C___ 2. Includes stepchildren.

___A___ 3. Includes two parents and biological and adopted children.

___G___ 4. Consists of a married couple without children who may focus on pursuing careers.

___D___ 5. Consists of a married couple pursuing careers while managing a family with children.

___E___ 6. Has grandparents living with the family.

___H___ 7. Has the challenge of explaining why the biological parents are not raising the child.

___B___ 8. Has fewer resources, such as time, energy, and money.

___C___ 9. Has the challenge of developing stepparent relationships.

___F___10. Has grandparents and relatives living nearby and taking part in family activities.

___D___11. Shares the role of earning income outside the home.

_A or C_12. Has one parent who may stay home as a full-time child caregiver.

A. nuclear family
B. single-parent family
C. stepfamily
D. dual-career family
E. extended family
F. modified extended family
G. childless family
H. adopting family

13. List six benefits of living in a family. Families provide for physical needs for food, clothing, shelter, and medical care; protection; long-lasting relationships; love and affection; support and encouragement; and companionship.

_____

_____

_____

14. Describe four functions of the family. Families socialize children, meet physical needs, meet emotional needs, and influence roles in society.

_____

_____

_____

Comparing Family Structures

Activity D

Section 14:3

Name _____

Date _____ Period _____

Choose two different family structures. In the space provided, compare and contrast them.

Comparison of Family Structures

Type of Structure: (Student response.)	**Type of Structure:** (Student response.)
Family composition: (Student response.)	Family composition: (Student response.)
Challenges of fulfilling the functions within this family structure: (Student response.)	Challenges of fulfilling the functions within this family structure: (Student response.)
Resources available to help family fulfill its functions: (Student response.)	Resources available to help family fulfill its functions: (Student response.)

Stereotypes and Singles

Activity E

Section 14:4

Name _____

Date _____   Period _____

Speech bubble (left): The weekend is here! Going to a party again tonight? Must be nice to be single—no commitments, no one to tell you what to do... you've got it made!

Speech bubble (right): Yeah, sure! No one to come home to, no one to share the rent, no one to eat supper with—by the time I get dinner made, eat, clean the house, do the laundry, and mow the lawn, I won't have much time left to do anything.

1. The conversation above shows stereotypes of a single person's life. Describe that stereotype. _Single people have no commitments, have a lot of freedom, and have a lot of fun._

   _____

2. In the conversation, what is the single person's point of view of single living? _Being single can be lonely. Also, when a person has to do all of the work of the home by himself or herself, there isn't much time for anything else._

3. What other stereotypes of single persons can you identify? _(Sample answers:) old maids, selfish, stingy, set in their ways_

   _____

4. How do stereotypes affect a person's image of himself or herself? How do they affect a person's self-esteem? _Stereotypes make it hard for a person to accept or like his or her self-image and can have a negative effect on a person's self-esteem._

   _____

Chapter 15

Strengthening Family Interactions

Roles in the Family

Activity A

Section 15:1

Name _____

Date _____ Period _____

Family members have various roles. The left column lists tasks that may be part of these roles. You may also think of other roles that family members have in your family. In the space on the right, identify each family member. Then list the tasks that go with that person's role in the family.   **(Student response.)**

Tasks	Family Member	Role Description
Buys a car		
Shops for clothes		
Shops for food		
Cooks meals		
Bakes cookies		
Picks up clutter		
Dusts furniture		
Vacuums rugs		
Sweeps floors		
Repairs small household items		
Makes doctor's appointments		
Chauffeurs		
Washes clothes		
Puts clothes away		
Calls repair person		
Fills the car with gas		
Maintains the car		
Mows the lawn		
Gardens		
Solves problems		
Organizes		
Gives instructions		
Acts as a peacemaker		
Serves as a listener		
Budgets money		
Pays bills		
Plans vacations		
Sets family rules		
Enforces family rules		
Reads to children		
Bathes young children		
Dresses young children		
Plays with children		
Earns household income		

Stages of the Family Life Cycle

Activity B   Name _____

Section 15:2   Date _____ Period _____

For each stage of the family life cycle, identify the changes that occur and describe the adjustments family members may need to make to maintain balance in the family system.

1. Newly Married Stage A couple marry and provide their own housing, food, and clothing. They take on new roles of husband and wife. The couple need to develop good communication patterns and learn to solve problems together. They need to set goals and plan for their future.

2. Early Parenthood Stage The tasks include caring for young children and meeting their needs. Parents need to understand child development and learn how to stimulate the young child's growth. Roles must be flexible. Having quiet moments together becomes a major need for a couple with young children.

3. Later Parenthood Stage The onset of puberty brings about rapid changes in physical growth and sexual development. The adolescent begins to appear more like an adult and less like a child. Parents must let go of some responsibilities, while teens take on more responsibilities.

4. Empty Nest Stage Parental roles change greatly. Children are no longer dependent on their parents for meeting their needs. As a child marries, parents need to accept the child's mate into the extended family. Parents may still provide some financial help or be involved in grandparenting.

5. Retirement Stage Couples enter the retirement stage after one or both spouses retire from their career. Some couples focus on themselves, hobbies, volunteer work, travel, or leisure activities. Some may lose self-esteem, or have health or financial problems.

6. Death of a Spouse The death of one partner ends the family life cycle. The remaining partner returns to single living, deal emotionally with the loss of a partner, and adjust to a lifestyle change. The loss of income, health, and the ability to live independently are hard to accept. Self-esteem may decline.

Building Strong Families

Activity C

Name _____

Section 15:3

Date _____ **Period** _____

Answer the following questions about family communication, decision making, and conflict management.

Communication

1. Name four ways family members can communicate to build esteem in each other.

   A. take time to talk to and listen to each other _____

   B. use active listening skills _____

   C. show respect for each other's viewpoints _____

   D. appreciate one another _____

2. Describe two actions you could take to improve communication in your family.

   A. (Student response.) _____

   B. (Student response.) _____

Family Decision Making

3. Describe *democratic decision making*. Group members take part in the selection of one choice and help to carry out the plan of action.

4. Give three examples of ways parents can teach children to develop decision-making skills.

   A. (Sample answers:) asking children to choose between two choices of acceptable clothing

   B. asking children to choose between two choices of vegetables for dinner

   C. allowing children to decide how to spend their time

5. In your own words, explain how sharing decision-making responsibilities in a family compares with sharing decision-making responsibilities in a business. (Student response should rephrase concepts on pages 335–336 in the text.)

Conflict Management

6. Give examples of two methods of helping a family member take ownership of a problem.

   A. (Student responses should include examples of using feedback and empathy.)

   B. _____

7. What is scapegoating? How does it affect the family system? Scapegoating is placing the blame for a problem on someone else. The self-esteem of the person who is wrongly blamed will suffer. Action isn't taken and problems don't get solved.

8. How does compromise help the family system maintain or return to a balanced state? Compromise is not a one-sided solution. Balance is restored because both sides give in a little.

Family-Strengthening Activities

Name _____

Date _____ Period _____

Think ahead about your own possible future family and consider some spontaneous (spur-of-the-moment) activities as well as those requiring advanced planning. In the space provided, identify one of each type of leisure activity for the following family members: **(Student response.)**

- yourself, as an individual
- one-on-one with a spouse
- one-on-one with a spouse or a child
- as a family unit
- with your extended family (grandparents and other relatives)

	Spontaneous	Planned
Individually		
With a Spouse		
With a Spouse or Child		
As a Family Unit		
With the Extended Family		

Chapter 16

Crises in the Family

The Pileup Effect

Activity A

Name _____

Section 16:1

Date _____ Period _____

Many life events bring changes and increase stress in a family. Read the list of stressful events below. Determine which single events and which combinations of events might lead to a family crisis. Then write your responses in the space provided below.

Stressful Life Event

Family moves to a new city

Member gets fired from job

Family goes on welfare

Family member goes to jail

Unmarried member becomes pregnant

Member starts a new business

Main wage earner becomes unemployed

Parents divorce

Mother spends more time away from home

Member becomes disabled

Family member becomes dependent on alcohol

Member makes a major purchase

Member changes to a new job

Conflicts between husband/wife increase

Arguments between parents and children increase

Family has to move to a different residence

Father spends more time away from home

A parent or spouse dies

A child dies

1. List below the single stressful event that you feel could lead to a family crisis. **(Student response.)**

   _____

   _____

   _____

   _____

   _____

2. List below three combinations of stressful events that you feel could lead to a family crisis.

   1. **(Student response.)**   1. _____   1. _____

   2. _____   2. _____   2. _____

   3. _____   3. _____   3. _____

The Family System and a Crisis

Activity B

Name _____

Section 16:1

Date _____ **Period** _____

Study the diagram below. Use it to examine how stressful events may cause the family system to become unbalanced.

The following situations would affect the family system. For each situation, identify the resources that would be lost and the needs that would increase. **(Chart includes sample answers.)**

	Lost Resources	Increased Needs
1. Mother loses her job.	money, self-esteem	meaningful work, self-esteem
2. Child goes to college.	time, energy, companionship	finances for college, new sources of friendship
3. Parents separate.	companionship, support, money	finances, friendship, child care, work of family
4. House is destroyed by a flood.	home, shelter, clothing, memorabilia	shelter, food, clothing, money, security, esteem
5. Teenager is in a car accident that results in permanent disability.	independence, money, personal esteem, worth	finances, time, health care, assistance for life, self-worth

The Grieving Process

Activity C

Name _____

Section 16:1

Date _____ Period _____

In the diagram, fill in the letters that correspond with the stages of the grieving process. Then, read the scenario below and answer the questions that follow.

- A. acceptance
- B. anger
- C. blame
- D. denial
- E. depression
- F. guilt

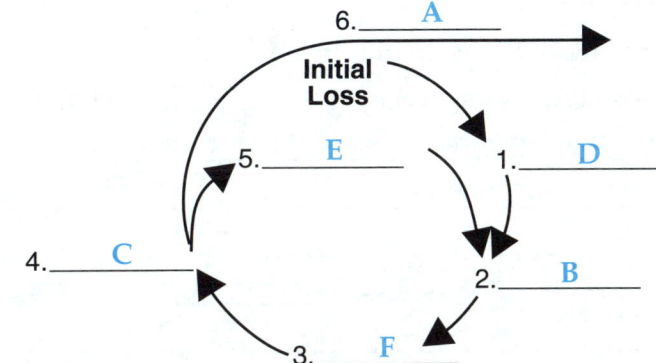

6. ___A___

Initial Loss

5. ___E___   1. ___D___

4. ___C___   2. ___B___

3. ___F___

Scenario: A teenager, driving too fast around a corner, loses control of the car and hits a tree. As a result, the car is totaled and the teenager becomes a paraplegic.

7. How might this crisis affect the family members' roles and resources? <u>Family members might have to help care for the teenager. The teen's roles will be reduced. Money will be reduced due to medical bills and car repair/replacement.</u>

_____

_____

8. What *healthy* adjustment pattern would return the family to a balanced system of functioning? Describe it. <u>(Sample answers:) taking a loan to help pay medical costs; hiring a full-time caregiver for the teen; taking time from work to help the teen adjust</u>

_____

_____

9. What *unhealthy* adjustment pattern would prevent the family from returning to a balanced system of functioning? Describe it. <u>(Sample answers:) refusing to accept the accident; not sharing time or resources; refusing to ask others for help</u>

_____

_____

_____

_____

_____

_____

Preventing a Crisis

Activity D

Section 16:2

Name _____

Date _____ Period _____

How can families handle stress and avoid a potential crisis? Developing family resources that help members meet their needs is one method that can help. Read each stressful event and respond to the questions that follow.

1. **Main wage earner becomes unemployed.**

   A. What is the family's viewpoint? What approach will help them handle this stressor?
   a family perspective that this is temporary, something they can handle, and something they can overcome together _____

   B. What is the source of the stress? _external, the former employer_ _____

   C. What can the family do to manage the stress? _have others work more, get a part-time job, apply for government assistance_ _____

   D. What resources can help the family handle the stress and avoid a potential crisis? _other family members, savings, unemployment compensation, government assistance_ .

2. **Child goes to college.**

   A. What family viewpoint will help members handle this stressor? _perceiving this as a desirable event, a step forward, and an exciting time_ _____

   B. What is the source of the stress? _internal change within the family, change in the roles family members take_ _____

   C. How can the family manage the stress? _by making adjustments at home, taking over the absent person's responsibilities, and parents taking the roles of encourager and supporter_ _____

(Continued)

D. What resources can help the family handle the stress and avoid a potential crisis?
good job, savings, a loan

3. **A grandparent who has a disability moves in with the family.**

A. What family viewpoint will help the members handle the stress and avoid a crisis?
seeing this step as a desirable action, something they can handle and want to do

B. What is the source of the stress? internal, requiring changes in the roles and responsibilities of family members

C. What steps can the family take to manage the stress? work together to meet the needs of the grandparent, share the responsibilities of providing care, focus on the enjoyment of having the grandparent in the home

D. What resources can help the family handle the stress and avoid a potential crisis?
affordable community or government services that can help the family meet needs

4. **A tornado destroys a family's home.**

A. What family viewpoint will help the members handle this stressor? recognizing that material things can be replaced as they rebuild and start over and being thankful that lives were spared

B. What is the source of the stress? external, the weather

C. What can the family do to manage the stress? work together to meet immediate family needs for shelter and food, seek help from others in the community or from extended family

D. What resources can help the family handle the stress and avoid a potential crisis?
Red Cross, insurance, family and community support

Managing a Crisis

Activity E   Name _____

Section 16:3   Date _____ Period _____

For each crisis-producing situation described below, list family needs that increase and are hard for members to fulfill. Then list the resources that become stretched under these increased demands. Finally, identify what family responses and what community resources can help members manage these situations. **(Chart answers are sample responses.)**

Crisis-Producing Situations

1. Chronic Illness in the Family

A. Family needs that increase:
health care services and equipment, finances to pay for the extra care, help with the roles that the ill family member used to do

C. Helpful family responses:
cooperation to work together, a focus on love and caring, help from extended family

B. Family resources that are stretched:
money and time, social relationships

D. Helpful community resources:
social services, health services, medical advances, educators, school psychologists

2. Drug and Alcohol Abuse

A. Family needs that increase:
emotional support, encouragement, good communication, joint decision making and problem solving

C. Helpful family responses:
cooperation, attitude of support and concern, positive attitude to seeking help

B. Family resources that are stretched:
money, emotional resources, family relationships

D. Helpful community resources:
law enforcement, social service, medical, and community services for abuser and victims

3. Criminal Attacks

A. Family needs that increase:
security, ability to cope with negative feelings, desire to see guilty person punished

C. Helpful family responses:
expression of feelings, focus on adjusting, rebuilding secure and stable attitudes

B. Family resources that are stretched:
need for support, aid, and nurturing from others they can trust

D. Helpful community resources:
law enforcement, social service, medical, and community services to help aid the victims

4. Moving

A. Family needs that increase:
new friends, places for recreation, places for religious worship, stores, new school, new job

C. Helpful family responses:
good communication, democratic decision making, an attitude of adventure and exploration, involvement in new community

B. Family resources that are stretched:
money, social resources, time focused on family members, family leisure time

D. Helpful community resources:
information centers, telephone book, neighbors, new coworkers, the Internet

Chapter 17

Divorce and Remarriage

The Effects of Divorce on the Family

Activity A   Name _____

Section 17:1   Date _____   Period _____

1. In the diagram boxes below, identify some possible roles for various family members.
   (Chart answers are sample responses.)

Father's Roles	Children's Roles	Mother's Roles
Provider of money and financial resources	Grow and develop to maturity	Provider of money and financial resources
Role model	Do well in school	Role model
Caregiver	Help in the work of the home	Caregiver
Companion for spouse and children	Provide friendship to one another	Companion for spouse and children
Emotional support for children and spouse		Emotional support for children and spouse
Shares in work of the home		Shares in work of the home

2. In the space below, draw two diagrams that show what could happen to the balance in a family system when there is a divorce. Include examples of how the parents' and children's roles have changed. Do the roles and responsibilities of each family member increase or decrease?

Parental Roles (Noncustodial Parent)	Parental Roles (Custodial Parent)	Children's Roles
provide financial resources for both households	has most of the parenting responsibilities	helping with work of the home
carry out all the household tasks such as cooking, cleaning, laundry	works and provides income	meeting some companionship roles for the single parents
still provides parenting when possible	does the work of the family at home	

(Continued)

3. What are four factors that could serve as barriers to divorce and keep a family from moving ahead with a divorce? **(List four:) want to keep their commitment to stay married until death; stay together for the children; avoid disapproval of family and friends; fear of being single; hope happiness of the past will return; fear they cannot afford to live alone**

_____

_____

4. Give an example for each factor that might contribute to a divorce in a marriage. Then explain what couples could do to (decisions they could make or skills they could develop) to help them avoid these factors in their relationship. **(Chart answers are sample responses.)**

Factor contributing to divorce	Example	How might couples avoid these factors in their relationship?
Differences in backgrounds	One partner wants to go to college and have a career; the other wants to stay in the community where he or she grew up.	Choose a mate with similar interests, goals, values
Immaturity	Either partner does not control emotional responses and related behaviors.	Work to grow and mature before choosing to marry
Poor relationship skills	Couples lie, don't talk openly and honestly, or blame each other for problems.	Develop skills for communicating, making joint decisions, and solving problems together
Problem situations	A couple marries because one partner cannot stand living at home any longer.	Develop skills for solving problems together and negotiating solutions
Financial conflicts	One partner spends more money than they can afford.	Develop skills for managing their money together
Teen marriages	A couple marries because they are pregnant.	Develop their personal resources and grow to maturity before choosing to marry

The Stages of Divorce

Activity B

Name _____

Section 17:2

Date _____   **Period** _____

The breakdown of a marriage relationship goes through three separate stages before the divorce is finalized. In the space provided, respond to the questions about each stage of this breakdown.

Stage One: Emotional Divorce

1. Describe the family situation during this stage. _Spouses stop sharing feelings and meeting_ _each other's emotional needs, then withdraw from each other._ _____

2. List examples of actions family members might take to try to restore balance within the family. _seeking counseling to rebuild and enrich their relationship, build communication and_ _problem-solving skills_ _____

Stage Two: Separation

3. Describe the family situation during this stage. _divided family structure, confusion,_ _loneliness, feelings of denial, anger, blame_ _____

4. List examples of actions family members might take to try to restore balance within the family. _seeking predivorce counseling to try to help the marriage, seeking divorce counseling to_ _get help with legal proceedings_ _____

Stage Three: Legal Divorce

5. Describe the family situation during this stage. _family is separated, finances are divided,_ _child custody arrangements are finalized, and family members may have to move_ _____

6. What adjustments must be made to meet the needs of family members and restore balance to the family system? _continuing to be involved in the children's lives, rebuilding self-esteem_ _and self-confidence, setting personal goals, getting new training if needed, adjusting_ _family roles so the work of the family is accomplished and financial needs are met_ _____

_____

_____

_____

_____

The Legal Divorce: Terms and Proceedings

Activity C   **Name**_____

Section 17:2   **Date** _____   **Period** _____

Research the legal procedures for divorce in your state. Then answer the following questions.

1. What is the residency requirement for divorce in your state? (Student response.)_____

_____

_____

_____

_____

_____

_____

2. What are grounds for divorce in your state? (Student response.)_____

_____

_____

_____

_____

_____

Match the following definitions with the appropriate terms.

_____G_____ 3. One parent provides the major share of child care.

_____I_____ 4. The spouse who did *not* file for the legal divorce.

_____D_____ 5. Valid reasons for obtaining a divorce.

_____B_____ 6. Payments that a noncustodial parent is required to pay toward the expenses of raising the children.

_____H_____ 7. Person who files for divorce.

_____F_____ 8. A divorce in which neither spouse is being blamed for the divorce.

_____K_____ 9. An arrangement for a noncustodial parent to visit the children.

_____A_____ 10. A financial settlement paid to a spouse.

_____E_____ 11. Both parents are required to share the rights and responsibilities of child care.

_____J_____ 12. The children are divided between the parents.

_____C_____ 13. The major responsibility for care of the children.

A. alimony
B. child support
C. custody
D. grounds for divorce
E. joint custody
F. no-fault divorce
G. one-parent custody
H. petitioner
I. respondent
J. split custody
K. visitation rights

Adjusting to Divorce

Activity D   Name _____

Section 17:3   Date _____   Period _____

1. Complete the chart below with examples of the changes that take place when a family goes through a divorce.   **(Chart answers are sample responses.)**

	Mother	Father	Children	Grandparents	Neighbors and Friends
Changes in Emotions	Angry, hurt, rejected, low self-esteem, lonely	Angry, hurt, low self-confidence, lonely	Angry, hurt, rejected, blame themselves, blame parents, insecure	Angry, worried, disappointed, concerned for children	Not certain what to do or say, uncertain, hurt, disappointed
Changes in Living Arrangements	Often single parent with custody of children	Often has to move and provide for both homes	Usually smaller than the home they had before the divorce	May feel obligated to help with moving, getting family settled	May be separated as the family moves away
Changes in Income	Has to provide for self and children, more expenses and less income	Has to provide for self and pay child support, may have more time if non-custodial parent	Often have to help with the work at home to make up for absent parent's roles in the work of the family	May feel they need to help with money, child care, opportunities for children	May not frequent the same places as before if friends cannot afford it
Changes in Parenting Arrangements	Often custodial parent	Often parent who has to pay child support	Split between parents, move between parents	Grandparents may not see children as much or may see more often	Children may not be around to play with neighbors and friends

(Continued)

2. What steps can the divorced adult take to adjust emotionally to the changes of a divorce? **Take time before looking for a new long-term relationship; rebuild self-esteem and self-confidence; find ways to grow and learn; take classes; develop personal skills.**

3. What steps can a divorced couple take to help their children adjust emotionally to the changes of a divorce? **Both parents should continue to be actively involved in their children's lives. Both need to spend time with each child, showing love and affection; both can show interest in the child's friends, achievements, and activities.**

4. Explain what the term *role overload* means for a single parent. **The single parent has too many roles and responsibilities to carry them all out well.**

5. What resources can help single-parent families with issues of role overload? **Grandparents, other family members, and friends may help with child care. In some cases, government aid can help with basic shelter, food, clothing, and health care.**

6. Many singleparents remarry and move their family into the stage of being a stepfamily. How does remarriage affect the balance between roles and responsibilities in the family system? **There are two parents to help balance out the work of the family, the roles of parenting and child care, and working to bring in finances.**

7. List four steps a stepfamily can take to help the family adjust to the changes in family structure.
   A. **Allow time for family unity to grow.**

   B. **Provide personal space for each family member.**

   C. **Make workable visitation arrangements for the absent parent and other people important to the children.**

   D. **Accept all family members in the stepfamily structure.**

Chapter 18

Families Change Over Time

The Aging Process

Activity A   Name _____

Section 18:1   Date _____ Period _____

Identify the changes of the middle years. Then identify changes of adolescence in the same areas.

	Middlescence (age 40-65)	Adolescence (age 12-19)
Physical Changes	Develop wrinkles, gray hair, slower reflexes, less stamina	Develop primary and secondary sex characteristics; develop strength and height as body matures
Emotional Changes	Question their purposes and goals; new emotions experienced as children grow up and leave home	Develop self-identity; question goals and purpose; learn to identify and control emotions
Social Changes	Become grandparents; focus on couple relationship; adjust to children leaving home; may become caregivers for aging parents	Look forward to leaving home; develop close relationships outside the family
Career Changes	Reach peak in career achievement; struggle with competition from younger employees; look ahead to retirement	Compete with peers for class rank, entry into colleges; look ahead to begin a career

1. What adjustments can help adults accept the changes that go with aging? revising goals or forming new goals; planning ahead for retirement; strengthening marital relationship; establishing close adult relationships with children

_____

2. How can understanding the similarities between midlife years and adolescent years help adults and teens adjust to the changes of these years? Knowing that all family members are going through similar changes should help families realize they need to communicate and solve problems together.

_____

Grandparenting

Name_____

Date _____ Period _____

Grandparents fulfill important roles in their grandchildren's lives. These roles fall into the four main areas shown below. For each area, think about the activities you do now with your grandparent(s) and list them in the appropriate areas of the top chart. Then complete the top chart by listing other activities you would enjoy doing with your grandparent(s). Finally, think ahead to what you could do as a grandparent to develop these roles in your grandchildren's lives. In the bottom chart, list three such activities in each space. **(Chart answers are student response.)**

Grandparenting Roles

Providing Focused Attention		Providing Child Care	
Activities we do now:	Other activities I would enjoy	Activities we do now:	Other activities I would enjoy
Continuing Family Traditions		Providing Financial Assistance	
Activities we do now:	Other activities I would enjoy	Activities we do now:	Other activities I would enjoy

My Future Roles as a Grandparent

Providing Focused Attention	Providing Child Care
Continuing Family Traditions	Providing Financial Assistance

The Retirement Years

Activity C

Name _____

Section 18:2

Date _____   Period _____

Complete the chart below by identifying the changes that take place during the retirement years for each area. Then identify things family members can do to help aging parents adjust to the changes of the retirement years.   (Chart answers are sample responses.)

Retirement		
Changes That Take Place	**How Changes Affect the Family System**	**How Family Members Can Help Adjustment to Change**
Changes in work roles	Nowhere to go; no schedule; less income; more time; may be a loss of self-esteem	Encourage the retired adult to develop hobbies and interests.
Changes in finances	May not be able to afford to do what they want	Encourage retirement planning. Apply for social security and Medicare benefits.
Changes in social life	More time, which is a valuable resource for helping family members	Help keep retired family members active. Involve them in your activities. Encourage them to be active in the community.

1. What are two recommendations that can help adults plan for an active retirement? maintain a positive attitude; stay healthy through diet and physical activity

_____

_____

2. How can adults plan to meet their financial needs after they retire? manage their money through the working years using savings and investments so they have an income during retirement; put money into a pension fund while working; apply for federal programs such as Social Security for assistance with income and Medicare for assistance with health expenses

Families Change Over Time

Activity D

Name _____

Section 18:3

Date _____ Period _____

Match the following terms with their definitions. Then write a sentence using the term.

adult day care   hospice care   pensions
agencies on aging   material abuse   retirement
community-based day care   Medicare   Social Security
elder abuse   middlescence   Supplemental Security Income
home health care   midlife crisis

agencies on aging   1. Local groups, such as Meals on Wheels, that bring many services to the elderly.
(Student response.)

home health care   2. Program in which nurses or aides go to the elderly person's home to provide assistance with health care.
(Student response.)

community-based day care   3. Programs usually held at senior centers with activities for independent older people.
(Student response.)

middlescence   4. The years between 40 and 65.
(Student response.)

elder abuse   5. Intentionally or knowingly causing an elder person to suffer.
(Student response.)

midlife crisis   6. Situation in which an adult views youthfulness as more desirable than aging and struggles with the adjustment.
(Student response.)

hospice care   7. Program that helps a dying person live the final days of life in comfort.
(Student response.)

pensions   8. Funds paid by employers to retired employees.
(Student response.)

material abuse   9. Misusing the elder person's property or financial resources.
(Student response.)

Supplemental Security Income   10. A federal program designed to help people who are age 65 or older, blind, or disabled with extra income.
(Student response.)

retirement   11. The ending of paid employment.
(Student response.)

Medicare   12. A federal program designed to help older people pay their medical bills.
(Student response.)

Social Security   13. A federal program designed to give retired people a source of income.
(Student response.)

adult day care   14. A program that transports older adults to centers that provide daytime group activities.
(Student response.)

Chapter 19

Choosing Your Career Path

Work and Your Lifestyle

Activity A   **Name** _____

Section 19:1   **Date** _____ **Period** _____

Explore your personal lifestyle expectations by answering the questions below.
(Answers are student response.)

1. In what geographic area do you plan to live? _____
   _____

2. Describe the type of home you expect to have. _____
   _____

3. What type of furnishings do you plan to purchase? _____
   _____

4. Describe the type of car you expect to buy. _____
   _____

5. Describe the hobbies or leisure activities you expect to pursue. _____
   _____

6. Describe the people you expect to have for friends. _____
   _____

7. Where do you plan to send your children to school? _____
   _____

8. Describe the type of vacation you expect to take each year. _____
   _____

9. What annual salary do you think it will take to support the above lifestyle? _____
   _____

10. Research career information materials to find out what types of jobs provide that level of
    income and list several. _____
    _____
    _____
    _____
    _____

Why Work?

Name _____

Date _____ Period _____

Each statement below represents one aspect of the many reasons why a person chooses a certain type of work. Match the statements in the left column to the appropriate reason in the right column.

___D___ 1. I want to be an artist because I see great beauty in my work.

___C___ 2. I want to go into physical therapy because the population is aging so many jobs will be available.

___G___ 3. I want to be an archaeologist so I can learn more about how society has changed.

___A___ 4. I want to be a surgeon because I want to earn a high salary.

___E___ 5. I want to be a medical researcher who finds a cure for AIDS.

___F___ 6. I want to be a builder because I feel good when I can see what I have made.

___A___ 7. I want to be a teacher so I can have summer vacations with my children.

___B___ 8. I want to be a plumber because I can receive training on the job.

___H___ 9. I want to be an entertainer so I have many friends.

___D___ 10. I want to be a mechanic because I like to work with machinery.

A. lifestyle
B. amount of training
C. high demand for that type of work
D. personal satisfaction
E. personal recognition
F. increase feelings of self-worth
G. provide an opportunity for personal growth
H. provide social contacts

Choose one career area that interests you. Write a paragraph addressing at least five of the above eight reasons (A-H) related to why people work.

I want to be a(n) (Student response.) _____ because

_____

_____

_____

_____

_____

_____

_____

_____

_____

_____

Your Personal Profile

Activity C

Name _____

Section 19:2

Date _____ Period _____

Complete the first three parts of this worksheet to help identify your personality, values, goals, interests, aptitudes, and abilities. Then, complete the fourth part by describing a job that fits your profile. **(Answers are student response.)**

Part One

In the space provided, list your favorite topics and hobbies.

Favorite Topics   **Hobbies**   **I Prefer to Work with**

(Check those that apply.)

_____ people

_____ words

_____ numbers

_____ objects (describe)

_____

_____

_____

Part Two

Check the career-related values and goals that are important to you.

Opportunities for

_____ challenge

_____ practical applications

_____ working independently

_____ leadership

_____ making money

Opportunities for

_____ recognition

_____ creativity

_____ working with people

_____ self-growth

_____ other values (describe)

_____

_____

Part Three

Circle the traits, aptitudes, and abilities below and at the top of the next page that best describe you. Then, in the space provided on the next page, list specific career-related skills you possess. (You may include additional skills not listed here.)

Physical	**Emotional**	**Social**	**Intellectual**	
active	sensitive	outgoing	investigative	numerical
moderate	self-disciplined	persuasive	orderly	verbal
quiet	calm	private	visionary	concrete
indoor	excitable	accepting	analytical	artistic
outdoor	reserved	independent	precise	realistic
	expressive		intuitive	

(Continued)

Aptitudes	Transferable Skills		Specific Skills
verbal	collecting data	helping	
numerical	sorting data	serving	
spatial	comparing data	leading	
physical dexterity	analyzing data	organizing	
	copying data	problem solving	
	teaching people	decision making	
	supervising	following directions	
	persuading	communicating in	
	negotiating	writing	

Part Four

Briefly describe two jobs that would fit your personal profile.

1. **(Student response.)** _____

_____

_____

_____

_____

_____

_____

_____

_____

_____

_____

2. **(Student response.)** _____

_____

_____

_____

_____

_____

_____

_____

_____

_____

_____

_____

_____

Career Research

Name _____

Date _____   Period _____

Choose a career cluster and pathway that interests you. Identify three occupations within the pathway that match your personal profile. If needed, refer to www.careerclusters.org. Research the occupations at your library or on the Internet, filling out the chart with your findings.

(Chart answers are student response.)

Career Cluster: _____

Pathway: _____

	Occupation #1 _____	**Occupation #2** _____	**Occupation #3** _____
Job Responsibilities			
Personality Traits Required			
Education and/or Training Required			
Skills Required			
Possible Employers			
Starting Income			
Working Conditions			
Advancement Opportunities			
Employment Outlook			

Career Terminology and the Career Clusters

Activity E

Section 19:2

Name _____

Date _____ Period _____

Match the following career-related definitions with the appropriate terms. Then answer the following questions.

____D____ 1. A series of jobs in which each builds on the experiences of the previous step.

____I____ 2. People who are self-employed and earn incomes through their own businesses.

____H____ 3. The United States' primary source of occupational information.

____A____ 4. Topics or activities that you enjoy.

____E____ 5. Beliefs or ideals that are important to you.

____K____ 6. What you would like to accomplish in life.

____C____ 7. Traits that affect the way you respond to your environment.

____J____ 8. Your natural talents.

____G____ 9. A position in which the worker learns skills and gains experience while under the supervision of an experienced worker.

____B____ 10. A collection of materials that document a person's achievements over time.

____L____ 11. A list of steps to take to reach a career goal.

____F____ 12. Skills that you learn and develop.

A. interests
B. portfolio
C. personality
D. career ladder
E. values
F. abilities
G. apprenticeship
H. O*NET
I. entrepreneurs
J. aptitudes
K. goals
L. career plan

13. Explain the difference between a job and a career. **A job is a position held by a person working to earn a living. A career refers to the work done over several years while holding different jobs.**

14. What are the career clusters? **Career clusters are 16 broad groupings of occupational and career specialties.**

15. How can the career clusters help you learn about careers? **The career clusters link school-based learning to career success. Each cluster includes several career directions, called** *career pathways*. **All the career choices within a pathway require a set of common knowledge and skills. The career clusters can help you determine what classes to take to prepare for a career within a certain cluster and pathway.**

16. Choose one career cluster and give an example of several jobs that could be part of that cluster. **(Student response.)**

_____

_____

Finding a Job

Activity F

Section 19:3

Name _____

Date _____ Period _____

Provide complete responses to the following items about finding a job.

1. List five sources of possible job leads. **(List five:) newspapers, online job listings, government employment offices, employment agencies, networking, friends, family members; membership in a professional organization**

_____

_____

_____

_____

2. What are two ways you can gather information about a job opening? **(List two:) Review the key requirements in the job posting; if no posting is available, try to identify the organization's needs through Internet or library research; talk to employees at the company; talk to people with a similar job.**

_____

3. Research the names and addresses of five potential employers for whom you would like to work. **(Student response.)**

_____

_____

_____

4. Choose one of the above employers. Arrange to interview an employee at the company. As part of the interview, find out about working conditions and employee benefits. In the space below, summarize your findings. **(Student response.)**

_____

_____

_____

_____

_____

_____

_____

_____

_____

_____

_____

Résumé and References Preparation Sheet

Activity G   **Name** _____

Section 19:3   **Date** _____ **Period** _____

Develop your own résumé by completing the information below. Then compile a list of references
to provide to employers upon request. **(Answers are student response.)**

Name: _____ Phone number: _____

Address: _____

E-mail Address: _____

Employment Objective: _____

_____

Education: _____

_____

_____

_____

Work Experience:

(Starting with the most recent, list each employer's name, address, and telephone number.)

_____

_____

_____

_____

Special Skills: _____

_____

_____

Honors and Activities: _____

_____

_____

References:

(List the names, addresses, telephone numbers, and e-mail addresses of three references whose
permission you have obtained.)

1. _____

_____

2. _____

_____

3. _____

_____

Preparing for an Interview

Activity H

Name _____

Section 19:3

Date _____ **Period** _____

Are you prepared for the types of questions you may be asked during a job interview? Interviewers commonly ask the questions that follow. Read each one and then write the response you would use during an interview.

Desired job: *(Student response.)* _____

1. What did you do at your last job? What were your responsibilities? *(Student response.)* _____

   _____

   _____

2. What parts of your last job did you like the best? *(Student response.)* _____

   _____

3. What aspects of your last job did you like the least? *(Student response.)* _____

   _____

4. For what reason did you leave your last job? *(Student response.)* _____

   _____

5. Why should I hire you for the job? *(Student response.)* _____

   _____

   _____

6. What would you want to be doing five years from now? *(Student response.)* _____

   _____

7. What are your main strengths? *(Student response.)* _____

   _____

8. What is your major weakness? *(Student response.)* _____

   _____

9. Tell me about your hobbies. What do you like to do in your spare time? *(Student response.)* ____

   _____

10. What do you do to manage stress in your life? *(Student response.)* _____

   _____

11. How long would you stay with us if this job were offered to you? *(Student response.)* _____

   _____

12. What else would you like to know about this job? *(Student response.)* _____

   _____

Chapter 20

Balancing Family and Work

Work Patterns

Activity A

Name _____

Section 20:1

Date _____ **Period** _____

Follow the individual directions for this three-part activity.

Part One: Diagram each work pattern below. Identify changes that take place between the beginning of the work years and retirement.

1. Conventional:

Begin Work ___ **Marriage** / **Child** / **Child** / **Child** / ___ Retirement

2. Career to family-focused:

Begin Work ___ / / **Marriage or Child (Stop Working)** / / ___ Retirement

3. Interrupted:

Begin Work ___ **Marriage or Child (Stop Working)** / **Child** / **Child** / **Begin Work Again** / ___ Retirement

(Continued)

Part Two: For each statement below, match the work pattern description with the appropriate work pattern. (Letters may be used more than once.)

___A___ 4. I do not plan to marry. I will work during my adult life whether or not I am responsible for the support of children.

        A. conventional

        B. career to family-focused

        C. interrupted

___C___ 5. If I marry, I will not work outside the home while our children are small. When the children are old enough for school, I will return to work.

___B___ 6. I will work after finishing school. If I marry, I will continue working outside the home until our first child is born, and then stop.

___C___ 7. I may leave the labor force for a short time. However, I may return again when I become responsible for the support of my children.

___A___ 8. If I marry, I still plan to continue holding a job even though I may have children.

___C___ 9. If I marry, I will not work outside the home while our children are living with us. However, once they leave home, I will return to work again.

Part Three: Match each of the following descriptions with the identifying term. Then answer the question that follows.

___E___10. The opportunity to be absent from work for a longer period of time to care for a young child.

        A flexible scheduling

        B. job sharing

        C. maternity leave

        D. paternity leave

        E. childrearing leave

        F. FMLA

        G. substitute child care

___G___11. Someone who will care for a child while parents are at work.

___A___12. The opportunity to choose hours of work, within reasonable limits.

___F___13. A law that allows workers to take leave for caring for children without fear of losing their job.

___C___14. The period when a mother is away from her job to give birth and recover from it.

___B___15. A full-time job split between two people.

___D___16. Time for a father to be away from his job following the birth of a child.

17. Explain why the above working conditions are considered "family friendly." **They allow parents to meet the financial needs of the family by working and earning money, yet they also allow parents to spend needed time caring for and meeting the needs of young children.**

_____

_____

Choosing a Work Pattern

Activity B

Section 20:1

Name _____

Date _____ Period _____

List the five factors that might have an impact on a person's choice of work pattern.
(Answers do not need to be in a certain order.)

1. goals and values _____

2. birth of children _____

3. employer policies _____

4. roles of family members _____

5. earning potential _____

Write a paragraph describing your thoughts, desires, dreams, or ideals as they relate to each of these factors. Include a description of the work patterns you would like to see in your future family.
(Student response.)

_____

_____

_____

_____

_____

_____

_____

_____

_____

_____

_____

_____

_____

_____

_____

_____

_____

_____

_____

_____

_____

_____

_____

Types of Substitute Child Care

Name _____

Date _____ Period _____

Define each type of child care arrangement listed below. Then list the benefits and limitations of each type.

	Definition	Benefits	Limitations
1. Child care in Child's Home	care provided in the child's home	reduce feelings of insecurity; often provided by relatives or close friends who are likely to have similar viewpoints about childrearing	may not provide a range of experiences for older children
2. Live-in Nanny	a person who cares for the child while living with the family	helpful for parents who work long hours, travel, or work irregular schedules; can provide consistent caregiving	cost can be high; important to have references
3. Family Child Care	care offered in caregiver's home	opportunities to play with other children; children from same family can be together; may offer flexible hours	should check to see that it is state licensed; may not have the variety of experiences a group child care may offer; may not have playmates of the same age for the child

(Continued)

	Definition	Benefits	Limitations
4. Group Child Care Center	centers where care for a fairly large number of children is provided	can interact with others the same age; offer educational programs with activities for children in all age groups; facilities and equipment are designed for children	hours may not suit work shift; important to check for quality care, group size, and child-staff ratios; individual attention may be scarce
5. Cooperative Child Care Center	organized, managed, and funded by parents who use the center	may be less expensive; parents have input into the practices at the center	parents may need to spend some time volunteering
6. Employer-Sponsored Child Care	funded by businesses for children of employees	is usually less expensive; hours will coincide with work schedule	not available through all employers

Children's and Parent's Needs for Quality Child Care

Activity D

Name _____

Section 20:2

Date _____ Period _____

If you were providing care for children of different age groups, what particular needs must you meet for each? Write your answers in the diagram. Then answer the question below.

1. Infant's Needs	2. Toddler's Needs
feelings of trust, security, make changes slowly, time for cuddling and holding, relaxed caregiver	secure environment, consistent care, one main caregiver, has need to explore environment, space to move about, a patient and flexible caregiver

3. Preschooler's Needs	4. Elementary Child's Needs
variety of experiences, opportunity to explore the environment, larger spaces to exercise, opportunities to play with other children	accountability, age-appropriate activities

5. What are the four primary needs of parents concerning child care? reasonable costs, availability when needed, a location close to work or home, quality child care

_____

_____

Chapter 21

Becoming a Leader in Your Community

Evaluate Your Style of Leadership

Activity A

Section 21:1

Name_____

Date _____ Period _____

What is your style of leadership? Read each of the following statements. Place a check in the *Usually* column if the statement applies to you most of the time. Place a check in the *Sometimes* column if the statement does not really describe you. If neither of the above responses applies to you, place a check in the *Never* column. When you finish, complete the evaluation below. **(Answers are student response.)**

Usually	**Sometimes**	**Rarely**	
_____	_____	_____	1. I like to work in structured situations.
_____	_____	_____	2. I like following guidelines to guarantee some measure of success.
_____	_____	_____	3. I like to be in control of a situation.
_____	_____	_____	4. Being productive is very important to me.
_____	_____	_____	5. I like to delegate responsibility.
_____	_____	_____	6. I prefer working situations that offer flexibility.
_____	_____	_____	7. I like to be creative in what I do.
_____	_____	_____	8. I prefer to be considered one of the group.
_____	_____	_____	9. I see people as being more important than the work that is being done.
_____	_____	_____	10. I am concerned that other people enjoy what they do.

To determine your style of leadership:

Count the total number of *Usually* responses you have for statements 1-5: _____

Count the total number of *Usually* responses you have for statements 6-10: _____

Statements 1-5 describe people with a task-oriented style of leadership. Statements 6-10 describe people with a relationship-oriented style. If you have checked several responses in both groups, you could likely lead either type of group with ease.

Which style of leadership best describes you? Explain. _____

_____

_____

_____

Choosing a Leadership Style on the Job

Activity B

Name _____

Section 21:1

Date _____ **Period** _____

Read each of the following job situations. Decide if the situation would require an authoritarian task-oriented style of leadership (place *A* in the blank) or relationship-oriented democratic style (place *R* in the blank). Explain your choice in the space provided. Would some situations require both types of leadership?

___A___ 1. A police chief divides the responsibilities for an investigation among several people. The chief assigns different jobs to each detective.

_____

___A___ 2. A surgeon instructs assistants on their responsibilities in an operation. There are no personal opinions expressed in a life-and-death situation.

_____

___R___ 3. A floor supervisor in a major department store finds the most efficient way to get the racks and shelves in order at the end of the business day. The floor supervisor seeks input from staff as to which method is most efficient.

___R___ 4. A high school principal implements a new schedule for teachers and students. If input is sought from the individuals involved, they will respond to the new schedule with greater support.

___R___ 5. A store manager's responsibility is getting personnel involved in carrying out the anti-theft policy throughout the store. If the store manager receives input from personnel and seeks their help in carrying out the policy, theft will likely decrease because employees are often the main problem in such thefts.

___R___ 6. A fast-food manager is responsible for reducing the amount of food wasted. Getting input from the staff for ideas to reduce waste will help the group work as a team.

___A___ 7. A shop foreman is responsible for decreasing safety hazards in the factory. Other than asking workers to identify any safety hazards they are aware of, the shop foreman needs to eliminate the safety hazards.

___A___ 8. A dock foreman's responsibilities include assigning loads and destinations to each truck driver that delivers for a distribution plant. The focus here is on the job, not on people's input.

___A___ 9. A nursing supervisor's responsibility is to make sure the assigned treatment for each patient has been administered. The supervisor will make sure treatments for each patient are to be administered by the staff.

___R___ 10. The chairman of the board for a cooperative child care center is responsible for developing a list of regulations for the center. The chairman accepts ideas from parents as to what regulations they would like in the center.

_____

What Makes a Group Successful?

Activity C   Name _____

Section 21:2   Date _____   Period _____

Match each characteristic below with one of the four qualities of successful groups that it illustrates.

___A___ 1. Members know what they are expected to accomplish.

___D___ 2. Members have a set meeting time.

___B___ 3. Members feel their input is important.

___D___ 4. Members know what their group's constitution stands for.

___C___ 5. Members have a quiet place where they can work in small groups.

___B___ 6. Members feel their contributions are accepted by others.

___A___ 7. Members feel like their time is well spent on worthwhile activities.

___C___ 8. Members have tables to work on during meetings.

___D___ 9. Members know their meetings start and end on time.

___B___ 10. Members in the group work together.

A. A successful group has goals.

B. A successful group is cohesive.

C. A successful group has an appropriate setting.

D. A successful group has structure.

Explain why it is important for group members to carry out each role listed below. Then give an example of what could happen if group members do *not* carry out these roles.

Group Member Roles	Importance	Example
A group member needs to be a clear communicator.	Group members need to understand each other to be effective.	(Sample answer:) Group members don't understand roles and responsibilities.
Group members need to be cooperative.	When group members cooperate, the group can achieve its goal.	(Sample answer:) Group members spend time arguing and don't achieve goals.
Group members need to be willing to participate.	All members need to participate to carry out the group's plan.	(Sample answer:) Only a few members participate and carry out the plans. The other members feel disconnected and leave the group.
Group members need to be able to control their participation.	Listening carefully and responding at appropriate times enhances group discussion.	(Sample answer:) One person dominates each discussion and other members don't share their opinions.

Which Law Applies?

Activity D　　　　　　　　　　　　　Name _____

Section 21:3　　　　　　　　　　　Date _____　Period _____

Laws are designed to protect the rights and safety of individuals as well as benefit society as a whole. In the top half of the page, read each situation and identify what type of law is violated by writing *state*, *federal*, or *local* in the blank spaces provided. Then provide complete responses to the statements that follow.

_____**state**_____　1. Speeding through a construction zone that has a posted speed limit of 45 miles per hour.

_____**federal**_____　2. Getting a chain letter in the mail asking you to send $1.00 to six people.

_____**federal**_____　3. A soldier is disabled by an accident that happens while he or she is on duty in the army.

_____**state**_____　4. A person is arrested for hit-and-run driving.

_____**federal**_____　5. A shipment of stolen goods is seized in Oregon, but the vehicle is registered in Texas.

_____**state**_____　6. A person fails to register and license a car in the state where he or she lives.

_____**local**_____　7. Failing to get a building permit when remodeling a house.

_____**state**_____　8. Failing to get a marriage license.

_____**local**_____　9. A fourteen-year-old, not accompanied by a parent, fails to be off city streets by midnight.

_____**state**_____　10. Passing a car on a road marked *no-passing zone*.

11. At the federal level, the lawmaking body is called the **U.S. Congress** _____.

12. Federal laws apply to **the entire country** _____.

13. Give four examples of situations in which federal laws apply: **(Give four:) spying, airplane hijacking, mail fraud, crimes affecting more than one state, military service, civil rights, misspending federal dollars**

14. Give six examples of situations in which state laws apply: **(Give six:) robbery, drunken driving, shoplifting, use of state funds, use of state highways, traffic laws, motor vehicle registration, marriage and divorce laws**

15. Local laws are called **ordinances** _____.

16. Give three examples of situations in which a local law applies: **zoning regulations, building codes, curfews**

Contractual Law

Activity E

Name_____

Section 21:3

Date _____   Period _____

Follow the individual directions for this two-part activity.

Part One: Each of the sections below are taken from a legal contract. Read each section and rewrite it in your own words.

1. In consideration of the sale to the undersigned, thereafter referred to as "buyer," by Electronics, Inc., thereafter referred to as "seller" of the following merchandise: stereo system, buyer agrees to be bound by the terms and conditions set forth in this instrument. (Sample answer:) The person buying a stereo system from Electronics, Inc. agrees to the terms and conditions of the contract.

2. Buyer shall pay to seller or its successors, or assigns the sum of $350 in monthly installments of $50, due and payable commencing June 1, 20XX, and thereafter on the first calendar date of each month, for a period of seven months. (Sample answer:) The buyer will pay $350 in monthly payments of $50 over a period of seven months, beginning with the first payment on June 1, 20XX.

3. Buyer hereby waives any demand for payment or notice of default. (Sample answer:) The buyer will not receive any payment reminders or notification of a missed payment.

4. For the purpose of securing payment of the obligation hereunder, seller reserves title and shall have a security interest in said merchandise until said amount is fully paid in cash. (Sample answer:) The seller officially owns the item until the buyer finishes making all payments.

5. In the event the buyer defaults in making any payment, the entire indebtedness shall become due and payable, together with any attorney's fees not exceeding twenty percent (20%) of the amount due. (Sample answer:) If the buyer misses a payment, the buyer must pay the full remaining amount due to the seller. In addition, the buyer must pay for any attorney's fees, up to 20% of the total amount due.

(Continued)

Part Two: A good friend asks you to lend her $200. Although she does have a job, you feel that she really needs the money to pay rent. She promises to pay you back in two months. You agree to lend her the money, but you want a written contract to cover your agreement.

Use the information given to write a contract that addresses the matter. **(Student response.)**

_____

_____

_____

_____

_____

_____

_____

_____

_____

_____

_____

_____

_____

_____

_____

_____

_____

_____

_____

_____

_____

_____

_____

_____

_____

_____

_____

_____

_____

_____

Chapter 22

Managing Your Time

Personal Daily Schedule

Activity A   Name _____

Section 22:1   Date _____   Period _____

Follow the individual directions for this two-part activity.

Part One: Note the way you spend your time over a three-day period. Record below your activities throughout each day. Then answer the questions that follow.

Personal Time Log

Time	Day 1	Day 2	Day 3
6–7 a.m.			
7–8 a.m.			
8–9 a.m.			
9–10 a.m.			
10–11 a.m.			
11–12 p.m.			
12–1 p.m.			
1–2 p.m.			
2–3 p.m.			
3–4 p.m.			
4–5 p.m.			
5–6 p.m.			
6–7 p.m.			
7–8 p.m.			
8–9 p.m.			
9–10 p.m.			
10–11 p.m.			
11–12 a.m.			
12–6 a.m.			

1. How much time did you spend on personal activities (eating, bathing, dressing, and sleeping)? **(Student response.)**
   _____

2. How much time did you spend on work activities (school, homework, and job)? **(Student response.)**
   _____

3. How much flexible time do you have in an average day? **(Student response.)**
   _____

4. In which areas could you better manage your time? Describe how. **(Student response.)**
   _____

(Continued)

Part Two: In the space provided, list the activities that are important to you in each area. Then answer the questions that follow.

Personal Activities	Relationship Activities	Work Activities	Leisure Activities	Support Activities

5. Looking at your use of time over the three-day period, how much total time did you spend on each of the five areas? **(Student response.)**_____

_____

_____

_____

_____

6. Overall, do you spend your time on activities that are important to you? Explain. **(Student response.)**_____

_____

7. Set one time management goal for the next week and write it down. **(Student response.)**_____

_____

_____

_____

8. Why do you think spending your time doing activities of personal value is important? **(Student response.)**_____

_____

Time Management and Goals

Activity B

Section 22:1

Name _____

Date _____ Period _____

Follow the individual directions for this four-part activity.

Part One: In the space provided, list three major goals on which you presently are working.

1. (Sample answer:) Becoming captain of the soccer team. _____
2. (Sample answer:) Scoring high enough on the ACT to meet college admission requirements. ___
3. (Sample answer:) Finding a summer job. _____

Part Two: Choose one of the above goals. Break it down into smaller subgoals and steps for reaching those subgoals.

Major Goal (Sample answer:) Finding a summer job. _____

A. Subgoal (Sample answer:) Find out what jobs are available in my community. _____

Step 1. (Sample answer:) Check online job postings for openings in my area. _____

Step 2. (Sample answer:) Check for job postings on community bulletin boards at the library, local stores, and town hall. _____

Step 3. (Sample answer:) Ask family and friends if they know about any job openings. ___

B. Subgoal (Sample answer:) Apply for jobs. _____

Step 1. (Sample answer:) Create a personal fact sheet. _____

Step 2. (Sample answer:) Create a résumé. _____

Step 3. (Sample answer:) Write cover letters as needed. _____

Part Three: Refer to Activity A to answer these questions.

4. Look back at your daily schedule in Part One. Do you spend at least some time every day working toward at least one of your goals? (Student response.) _____

5. Look back at question #3. How much flexible time did you have in a day? (Student response.) ___

Part Four: Based on what you have learned in this activity about your time management, answer the following question.

6. How could you manage your time differently to make better progress toward reaching a goal? (Student response.) _____

_____

_____

_____

_____

_____

My Time Management Plan

Name _____

Date _____   Period _____

(Students should use the chart below to develop a time management plan for one week.)

My Weekly Time Management Plan

Dates: _____ to _____

Most Important Activities:

Deadlines:

Least Important Activities:

Deadlines:

	Sunday	Monday	Tuesday	Wednesday	Thursday	Friday	Saturday
To-Do List:							
Goals for Today							
Time Schedule							

Chapter 23

Managing Your Money

Understanding Your Paycheck

Activity A   Name_____

Section 23:1   Date _____   Period _____

Follow the individual directions for this two-part activity to show your understanding of employee earnings, deductions, and paychecks.

Part One: Ryan Swanson worked 40 hours at $12.00 per hour and four additional hours at time-and-a-half. He claimed one exemption for income tax withholding. Figure his deductions and take-home pay in the work area below.

Paycheck Worksheet

Total hours worked: _____44_____

Regular hours	40	× regular hourly pay	$12.00	= $	480.00
Overtime hours	4	× overtime hourly pay	$18.00	= $	72.00
			Total gross pay = $		552.00

Deductions:

Social Security (6.2%)	= $	34.22
Medicare tax (1.45%)	=	8.00
Federal withholding tax (about 9.4%)	=	51.89
State withholding tax (varies, estimate 4%)	=	22.08
Total deductions:	=	116.19
Net take-home pay:	= $	435.81

Part Two: Write a check to Ryan showing the correct take-home pay.

Coastal Cannery   054321
West Coast Road   **February 17, 20XX**
West Coast, WA 01234

Pay To The
Order Of_____Ryan Swanson_____ $ 435.81

_____Four hundred thirty-five and ⁸¹⁄₁₀₀_____ Dollars

1st Bank of West Coast   (student's name)
West Coast, WA 01234   _____

Sources of Income

Name_____

Date_____   Period_____

The situations below describe income earned from six different sources. Figure the amount of income earned in each situation and write the figure in the appropriate space.

1. Hourly Wage: $8.50 _____

   Joseph worked 35 hours this week as a checkout clerk at the grocery store. He earns $8.50 an hour. How much was his gross pay? $297.50 ($8.50 × 35) _____

   _____

2. Salary: $32,500 _____

   Karen works as a display manager for a large department store. She earns a salary of $32,500 a year. She gets paid twice each month. How much is her gross pay each paycheck? $1354.17 ($32,500 ÷ 12 = $2708.33 ÷ 2) _____

   _____

3. Commission: 3% _____

   Laurel earns a commission of 3 percent on each house she sells as a real estate agent. She sold a house for $189,500 this month. What was the gross amount of her commission check? $5,685 ($189,500 × 3%) _____

   _____

4. Business sales: $4,200 _____

   As an entrepreneur, Alec runs a small business printing labels for a packaging company. This month, his total sales were $4,200. His total expenses were $1,080. How much profit did he make? $3,120 ($4,200 − $1,080) _____

   _____

5. Savings: $120 _____

   Robert has $120 in his savings account. He left it in for one year at 3 ½ percent interest. How much was his interest income for that year? (Figure it as simple interest.) $4.20 ($120 × 3.5%) _____

   _____

6. Investment: $200 a month _____

   When he turned 25, Lin started investing in a retirement account. If he deposits $200 a month until age 65, how much money will he have contributed to the account? $96,000 ($200 × 12 months = $2,400/year; $2,400 × 40 years = $96,000) _____

   _____

Planning a Budget

Activity C

Name _____

Section 23:2

Date _____ Period _____

Refer to the scenario on page 503 in your text as you complete the following activity.

1. How much net income do Hans and Britta have to budget monthly?

    A. Gross monthly income = $ <u>2,550</u>

    B. School loans = $ <u>5,000</u> divided over 12 months = $ <u>416.67</u> /month

    C. Deductions per month = $ <u>626 ($222 + $160 + $244)</u>

    D. Net monthly income = $ <u>2,340.67 ($2,550 + $416.67 = $2,996.67 – $626)</u>

2. How much should they put in savings each month to cover car repairs? (Assume their expenses will be the same as last year.) $ <u>28.33 ($340 ÷ 12 months)</u>

3. How much should they put in savings each month for car insurance? $ <u>75 ($900 ÷ 12 months)</u>

4. Using the form below, prepare a budget for Hans and Britta. Use the amounts they have set aside for fixed and variable expenses and savings.

Monthly Budget

Fixed Expenses		Variable Expenses	
Rent	$690	Food	$400
Health Insurance	$110	Utilities	$150
Fixed expense total:	$800	Clothing	?
		Gas/Oil	$135
		Bus fare	$90
Savings		Entertainment	$50
Car Insurance fund	$75	Gifts	?
Emergency fund	$28.33	School expenses	
Tuition	$400	(Books, fees, supplies)	$125
Savings total:	$503.33	**Variable expenses total:**	$950

Total expenses: (fixed + variable + savings) $ <u>$2,253.33</u>

5. After figuring their total expenses, how much income do they have remaining? <u>$87.34</u>
(net income – total expenses)

6. Where would you suggest they put the remainder of their income? Explain your answer.
(Student response.)

_____

_____

_____

7. Follow the suggested guidelines recommended by the financial advisor in the scenario. Fill in the amounts below.

Expenses	Recommended Percentages		Net Income		Recommended Total	Budget Actual Amount
Rent	28%	×	$2,340.67	=	$655.38	$690
Utilities	9%	×	2,340.67	=	210.66	150
Food	18%	×	2,340.67	=	421.32	400
Transportation and auto insurance	15%	×	2,340.67	=	351.10	328.33 *Add all transportation expenses*
Entertainment	5%	×	2,340.67	=	117.03	50
Clothing	4%	×	2,340.67	=	93.63	0
Gifts	3%	×	2,340.67	=	70.22	0
Household items	5%	×	2,340.67	=	117.03	0
Education/reading	2%	×	2,340.67	=	46.81	525
Health care and miscellaneous	5%	×	2,340.67	=	117.03	110
Savings	6%	×	2,340.67		140.44	0

Use the form above to compare Hans' and Britta's budget with the financial advisor's suggested budget. Then answer the questions below.

8. In which areas do Hans and Britta spend more than the average? rent and education/reading

_____

_____

_____

9. In which areas do they spend less than average? utilities; food; transportation and auto insurance; entertainment; clothing; gifts; household items; health care and miscellaneous; savings

_____

10. Do you think Hans and Britta could continue with this budget long term? Explain your answer. (Student response.)

_____

_____

11. In which areas are expenses likely to increase over a period of time? Why? Eventually, their car will need to be replaced. Their clothing will wear out. Expenses for household items will increase. They also need to start saving for emergencies.

_____

_____

Opening a Checking Account

Activity D

Name _____

Section 23:3

Date _____ Period _____

Obtain brochures describing the checking accounts offered at three different financial institutions. You may also use the Internet to visit the financial institution Web sites. Complete the chart with the information you learn. Then answer the following question.   **(Chart answers are student response.)**

Name			
Location			
Hours			
FDIC/NCUA insured	☐ Yes ☐ No	☐ Yes ☐ No	☐ Yes ☐ No
Minimum deposit to open			
Minimum balance			
Interest earned			
Service fees			
Debit/ATM card available	☐ Yes ☐ No	☐ Yes ☐ No	☐ Yes ☐ No
Online banking	☐ Yes ☐ No	☐ Yes ☐ No	☐ Yes ☐ No
Overdraft protection	☐ Yes ☐ No	☐ Yes ☐ No	☐ Yes ☐ No
Overdraft fees			
Check ordering fees			

If you were opening a checking account, which of these financial institutions would you choose? Explain. **(Student response.)** _____

_____

_____

_____

_____

_____

Credit Terms and Protection

Activity E

Name _____

Section 23:4

Date _____ Period _____

Answer the following questions relating to using credit.

1. Define *revolving credit*. A type of credit that allows a person to continuously borrow and repay money, within the credit limit.

2. Give two examples of common uses for revolving credit. (Sample answers:) furniture, vacations, appliances, clothes

3. Define *installment credit*. A type of credit that is repaid in equal installments over a set period of time.

4. Give two examples of common uses for installment credit. (Sample answers:) car, house, education, new business

5. List four advantages of using credit. buy goods that you don't have the cash to pay for; buy goods and services when needed; convenient; safer than carrying large amounts of cash.

6. List four disadvantages of using credit. unplanned spending; spending too much; overusing credit; misusing may result in losing items purchased or repossession; interest costs.

Match the characteristics of credit described below with the appropriate terms.

_____H_____ 7. The annual cost of credit

_____C_____ 8. A record of how well you paid your bills in the past.

_____B_____ 9. Requires that lenders disclose the exact cost of using credit.

_____F_____ 10. Gives a consumer the right to verify the information in his or her credit report.

_____I_____ 11. The maximum amount of money a person can borrow on a credit card.

_____E_____ 12. A type of credit that allows a person to continuously borrow and repay money, within a credit limit.

_____D_____ 13. A type of credit, such as a loan, that is repaid over time in equal payments.

_____A_____ 14. States that certain factors such as race, color, sex, and marital status cannot be used to determine whether credit is granted.

_____G_____ 15. A form of security on a loan.

A. Equal Credit Opportunity Act

B. Truth in Lending Act

C. credit rating

D. installment

E. revolving

F. Fair Credit Reporting Act

G. collateral

H. annual percentage rate (APR)

I. credit limit

Chapter 24

Protecting Your Resources

Types of Advertising

Activity A

Section 24:1

Name_____

Date _____   Period _____

Six types of advertising methods are listed. For each type, find and attach an ad that illustrates the method. In your own words, explain how each ad tries to convince you to buy a product.

Factual Information	Product Comparison
(Student response.)	(Student response.)
How does this ad try to convince you to buy a product?	How does this ad try to convince you to buy a product?

(Continued)

## Endorsement (Student response.) How does this ad try to convince you to buy a product?	## Attention-Getter (Student response.) How does this ad try to convince you to buy a product?
## Association (Student response.) How does this ad try to convince you to buy a product?	## Emotional Appeal (Student response.) How does this ad try to convince you to buy a product?

Informed Purchasing

Activity B

Name _____

Section 24:1

Date _____ **Period** _____

Identify a product that you would like to buy. Then compare two different brands or two stores to determine which offers the best buy. Consider all aspects below and any others you may identify. Fill in the chart with the results of your comparison. Then answer the question that follows. **(Answers are student response.)**

Item you want to buy: _____

Characteristics	Brand/Store A	Brand/Store B
Quality		
Expected Performance		
Size		
Price		
Warranty		
Ease of Service		
Safety		
Ease of Use		
Results of an Independent Testing Organization		
Opinions of Friends or Family		

Which product do you feel would be the best buy? Explain your choice. _____

_____

_____

Insurance for the Family

Activity C

Section 24:2

Name _____

Date _____ Period _____

1. Define the following:

   A. Insurance: a form of protection against financial loss
   _____

   B. Premium: a fee paid to an insurance company for them to assume a financial loss that is described in the policy

   C. Policy: a contract between the insurance company and the policyholder

   D. Liability: the legal responsibility for another person's financial costs due to a loss or injury

2. Brainstorm and list risks that a family might have for potential losses.
   (Chart answers are sample responses.)

Possible property loss risks:	Possible liability risks:
home—fire, storms	damage to someone else's property
furnishings—fire, flooding, theft	damage to someone else's car
landscaping—vandalism, storms	others hurt by my personal property
jewelry—theft	others hurt by my pet
clothing—theft, storms	others hurt on my property
Possible financial risks:	**Possible personal risks:**
loss of job	loss of health
theft of money	injury so I cannot work or take care of myself
loss of investments	chronic illness so I cannot work or take care of myself
decrease in property value	death of a family member

3. In your lists above, circle or highlight the areas that would affect you the most if you should experience that loss in your family this week. (Student response.)

4. How would you decide how many types of insurance you need to carry? (Student response.)
   _____
   _____

Car Insurance

Name _____

Date _____   Period _____

Read the following scenario. Then analyze the automobile policy below and answer the questions that follow.

Molly is a 21-year-old female. She was driving a friend when she had an accident with another car, a BMW, that was carrying two passengers. Molly and her friend went to the hospital and were checked out with minor injuries. Both people in the other car were taken to the hospital in an ambulance, and the other car was damaged beyond repair. The estimate to fix Molly's car was $8,000. The accident was clearly Molly's fault. Molly had taken out the following automobile policy:

Bodily Injury/Property Damage:	50/100/50
Uninsured Motorists:	50/100
Underinsured Motorists:	50/100
Medical Payments:	1,000
Collision:	250 deductible
Comprehensive:	250 deductible
Car:	2003 Dodge Neon, 4 cylinder, sedan, 4 door SE
Driver:	Principal driver, age 21, female, single, no dependents. Pleasure travel only, 7500 miles annually No violations or accidents in last 3 years
Semi-annual premium:	$598

1. What is the maximum amount the insurance company will pay for the doctor and hospital bills that Molly might have? **$1,000** _____

2. What is the maximum amount the insurance company will pay for all the injuries of the driver of the other car? **$50,000** _____

3. What is the maximum amount the insurance company will pay for all the injuries to Molly's friend and the passengers in the BMW? **$100,000** _____

4. What is the maximum amount the insurance company will pay towards the repairs of the BMW? **$50,000** _____

5. How much money will Molly have to pay out-of-pocket if she decides to have her car repaired? **$250** _____

6. If Molly's car is not worth the $8,000 that it takes to repair it, how much will the insurance company pay her for the damage to her car? **the value of the car minus the $250 deductible**

(Continued)

7. How much money does Molly need in her monthly budget to cover her car insurance expenses?
$598 ÷ 6 = $99.67
_____

_____

8. Do you think Molly has enough coverage in her car insurance policy? Explain your answer.
(Sample response:) No. $100,000 is not enough to cover possible medical fees for four

people.

_____

_____

_____

_____

_____

9. Research the minimum liability requirements for automobile insurance in your state. (You can find a link to your state's Department of Insurance through the Insurance Information Institute's Web site, www.iii.org, under Media/Directories/Listings by State/Insurance Departments. (Student response.)

Bodily Injury/Property Damage: _____/_____/_____

Uninsured Motorists: _____/_____

Underinsured Motorists: _____/_____

Medical Payments: _____

10. If Molly had only carried the minimum liability requirements in your state, would she have had enough coverage to protect her from losses due to her accident? (Student response.)_____

_____

_____

_____

_____

_____

_____

_____

_____

Invest with Knowledge

Name_____

Date _____   Period _____

Match the following investment terms with their definitions.

____B____ 1. A written pledge by corporations or governments to pay back money plus interest to investors in a certain period of time.

____N____ 2. A type of investment sold by the federal government to finance government activities.

____E____ 3. A person trained to advise people on making wise investments.

____C____ 4. A type of investment sold by businesses to finance business activities.

____O____ 5. The Treasury Department of the federal government issues these secure investments through banks and other financial institutions.

____M____ 6. Shares in the ownership of a company.

____F____ 7. An increase in the general level of prices.

____D____ 8. Money paid to stockholders out of the company's earnings.

____J____ 9. A group of many investments purchased by a company representing many investors.

____H____ 10. A type of mutual fund that invests in short-term high-yield securities.

____K____ 11. A type of investment property such as a home, land, or rental property.

____L____ 12. People who buy stock in a company.

____G____ 13. An individual retirement account that helps increase financial security for older adults.

____A____ 14. A type of investment that provides guaranteed income for life.

____I____ 15. A type of investment sold by local governments to finance community projects.

A. annuity
B. bond
C. corporate bonds
D. dividend
E. financial planner
F. inflation
G. IRA
H. money market fund
I. municipal bonds
J. mutual fund
K. real estate
L. stockholder
M. stocks
N. U.S. government bonds
O. U.S. savings bond

Making Sound Investments

Activity F   Name _____

Section 24:3   Date _____ Period _____

Read each of the following investment situations and state if you agree or disagree with the person's choice of investment. Explain your answer. Then suggest a different investment opportunity for each and explain your reasoning.

1. Walisha has saved $5,000 in her savings account. Her job seems to be secure so she decides to buy $5,000 worth of stock in a company with a reputation for future growth. **(Sample response:) I disagree because even with a seemingly sound company, stocks can be a risky option.**

   _____

   _____

   Suggest another investment option: **(Student response.)** _____

   _____

   _____

   _____

2. Jacque would like to put $200 per month in an investment that earns more money than the savings account he presently has, which totals $3,000. He wants to save money for a down payment on a house he hopes to buy in five years. He decided to buy U.S. savings bonds that would mature around the date he plans to buy a home. **(Sample response:) I disagree, because savings bonds will not earn that much interest in the relatively short period of five years.**

   _____

   Suggest another investment option: **(Student response.)** _____

   _____

   _____

   _____

3. Maria received a gift of $1,000 for her newborn baby. She wanted to invest the money in a secure investment, yet earn enough interest to help pay her child's college tuition. She decided to put the money in a mutual fund. **(Sample response:) I agree, because the money will be invested in a variety of investments, so losses are likely to be balanced with gains.**

   _____

   _____

   Suggest another investment option: **(Student response.)** _____

   _____

   _____

   _____

Family Protection and Security

Activity G

Section 24:3

Name_____

Date _____   Period _____

Crossword grid (filled answers):

- 1 Across: PERILS
- 2 Down: LIABILITY
- 3 Across: CORPORATE
- 4 Down: POLICY
- 5 Down: ESTATE
- 6 Down: WUNIVERSAL
- 7 Across: TRUST
- 8 Across: MUNICIPAL
- 10 Across: CASH
- 11 Down: HMM
- 12 Across: LABELS
- 13 Down: ANNUNU...
- 15 Across: CONSUMER
- 16 Across: BOND
- 17 Down: BENEFIT
- 18 Down: DEDUCTIBLE
- 19 Across: REAL ESTATE
- 20 Across: WHOLE LIFE
- 21 Down: DIFFY...
- 22 Down: PP...
- 23 Down: W
- 24 Down: STOCKHOLDERS
- 25 Down: LIFE
- 26 Across: DEATH
- 27 Across: TESTIMONIAL
- 28 Down: S
- 29 Down: FACEVALUE
- 30 Across: INSURANCE
- 31 Across: INDEPENDENT
- 32 Down: TERM
- 33 Across: EMERGENCY
- 34 Across: MONEY
- 35 Down: FACE
- 36 Down: RIDER
- 37 Across: SAFE DEPOSIT
- 38 Across: PREMIUM

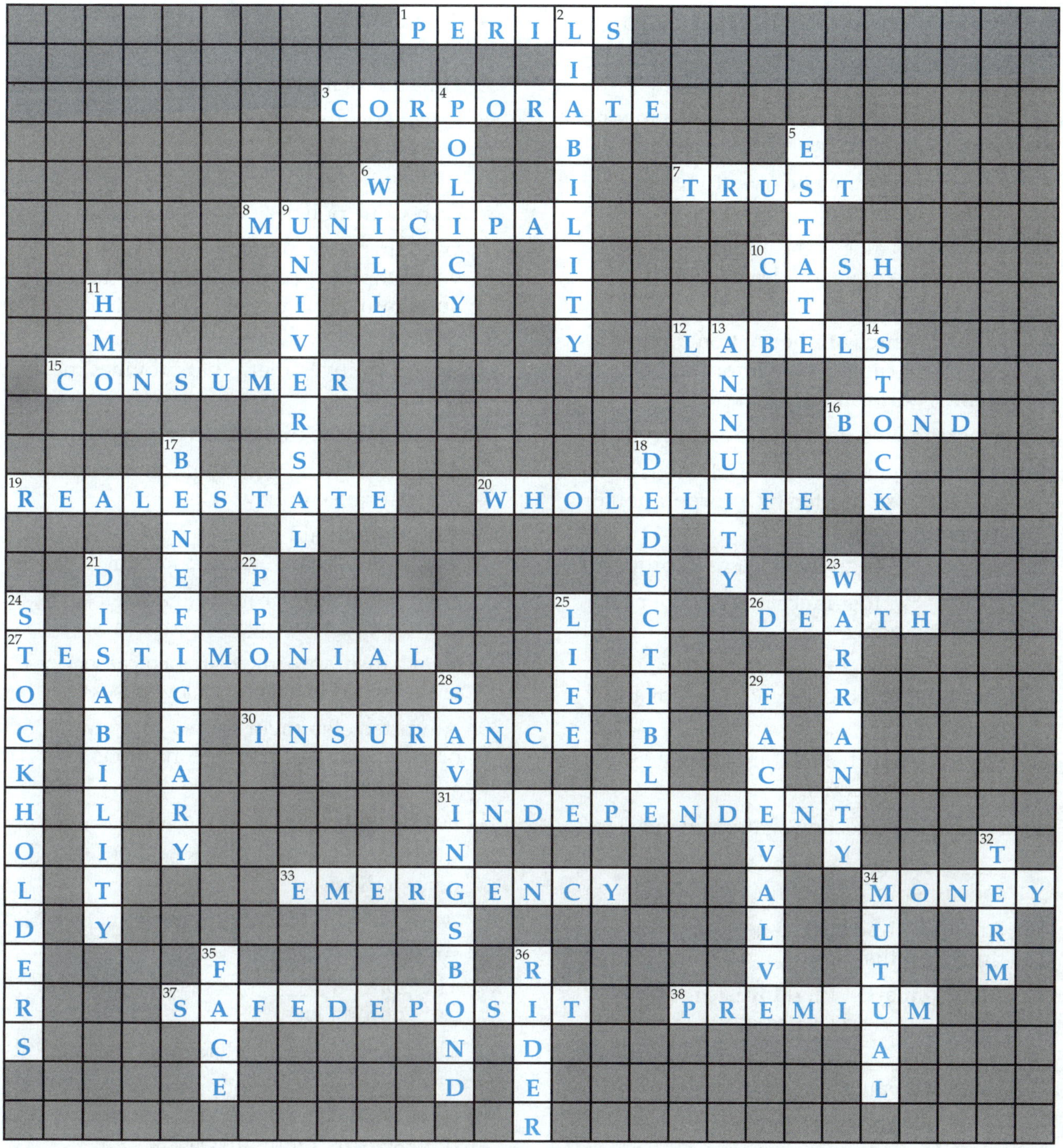

(Continued)

Read the descriptions and decide which chapter terms are being described. Write the correct terms in the crossword puzzle.

Across

1. Dangers such as an accident or a storm that cause a loss.

3. Corporations sell _____ bonds to finance business.

7. Permits the transfer of property or income from you to a second group for the benefit of your beneficiaries.

8. A _____ bond may be used to finance a library or a school.

10. The _____ value is the amount you get if you drop or surrender a whole life insurance policy.

12. A good source of information found on a product; can provide information on quality, performance, and price.

15. A person who uses goods and services.

16. A written pledge to pay back money plus interest, written by a corporation or government agency.

19. _____ _____ is an investment in property.

20. _____ _____ insurance is a form of cash value insurance.

26. The _____ benefit from life insurance should match the survivor's needs for money.

27. An ad in which a famous person endorses a product.

30. A form of protection against financial loss.

31. _____ testing organizations provide consumer information.

33. An _____ fund should be equal to at least three months income.

34. A _____ market fund invests in short-term high-yield securities.

37. A _____-_____ box is a storage area in a vault in a bank.

38. A fee charged by a company that provides insurance.

Down

2. The legal responsibility for another person's loss.

4. A contract between the insurance company and you.

5. The sum of all your personal property.

6. A legal document stating a person's wishes after death.

9. _____ life insurance combines term and cash value policies.

11. With this type of health insurance plan, your employer pays a monthly amount to an organization of medical personnel and facilities.

13. A type of investment that provides income for life.

14. A share in the ownership of a company.

17. The person who gets the money from a life insurance policy.

18. An amount paid by the policyholder on a loss before the insurance company pays.

21. _____ insurance protects against loss of income due to an accident or illness.

22. Health insurance in which medical services are provided to groups for lower fees.

23. A written statement from a company or manufacturer giving conditions for service or repair.

24. People who buy stock in a company.

25. Insurance that provides a benefit when a person dies.

28. A _____ _____ is a secure investment with the U.S. government.

29. The policy's _____ _____ is the most you can get for a loss.

32. Life insurance provided for a set time period.

34. A _____ fund is a group of many investments purchased by a company representing many investors.

35. The _____ amount is the amount of insurance purchased.

36. Extra protection may be added to a policy as a _____.

Meeting Your Nutritional Needs

Your Eating Habits

Activity A

Name _____

Section 25:1

Date _____   **Period** _____

Think about your eating habits. For each question, check the answers that best describe what, how much, when, where, and why you eat. After you have completed the checklist, respond to the statement that follows. **(Answers are student response.)**

1. What foods do I usually eat?

_____ Breads	_____ Fish
_____ Cereals	_____ Milk
_____ Rice	_____ Yogurt
_____ Pasta	_____ Cheese
_____ Vegetables	_____ Fast-food entrees
_____ Fruits	_____ Soft drinks
_____ Meat alternatives (eggs, dry beans, peanut butter)	_____ Sweets such as candy, cookies, or cakes
_____ Meats	_____ Snacks such as potato chips, corn chips, or pretzels
_____ Poultry	

2. How much do I usually eat?

_____ As much as I can hold (large servings)

_____ Enough to just feel full (small servings)

3. When do I usually eat?

_____ Anytime

_____ At mealtime only

_____ After school

_____ When I watch TV or study

_____ When I'm with friends

(Continued)

Name_____

4. Where do I usually eat?

_____ At home, at the kitchen or dining room table

_____ In front of the TV or elsewhere in the house

_____ At restaurants

_____ At school

5. Why do I usually eat?

_____ I'm hungry

_____ It's time to eat

_____ Everyone else is eating

_____ I'll hurt the cook's feelings if I don't eat

_____ I'm bored

_____ The food looks tempting

_____ I'm lonely

Review the sources of the six nutrients. Then write a paragraph describing how your eating habits have the potential to meet your needs for each nutrient. Also identify areas where your eating habits do *not* help you meet the needs for each nutrient. __(Student response.)_____

_____

_____

_____

_____

_____

_____

_____

_____

_____

_____

_____

_____

_____

_____

_____

_____

_____

_____

_____

_____

Nutrients and Their Functions

Activity B

Name _____

Section 25:1

Date _____ Period _____

Fill in the blank with a term that matches each description.

____carbohydrates____ 1. Provide the body with a major source of energy.

____sugar____ 2. A quick source of energy found in foods such as fruit, honey, and molasses.

____starches____ 3. A complex carbohydrate found in breads and cereals.

____fiber____ 4. Aids in digestion and found in cellulose and gums.

____fats____ 5. Maintain healthy skin and cell membranes and protect body organs.

____cholesterol____ 6. A fat that helps the liver make bile, vitamin D, and sex hormones.

____saturated fats____ 7. The fatty acids present in meats and dairy products.

____unsaturated fats____ 8. The fatty acids found in fish oils and olive oil.

____protein____ 9. Builds and repairs body cells.

____enzymes____ 10. Proteins that direct chemical reactions in the body, including digestion.

____antibodies____ 11. Proteins that fight off disease.

____minerals____ 12. Inorganic elements found in the earth's crust that are vital, in small amounts, for the proper functioning of the body.

____calcium____ 13. A mineral needed to avoid osteoporosis, a disease of porous bones.

____iron____ 14. A mineral needed to build new red blood cells and carry oxygen in the blood.

____vitamins____ 15. A nutrient involved in regulating the action that takes place in cells, affecting growth, reproduction, digestion, and overall health.

____water soluble____ 16. Vitamins that cannot be stored in the body and must be present in the diet every day.

____B vitamins____ 17. Vitamins that contribute to healthy nerves, appetite, digestion, and red blood cells.

____vitamin C____ 18. A vitamin that helps the body fight infection and heal wounds.

____fat-soluble____ 19. Vitamins that can be stored in the body.

____vitamin A____ 20. A vitamin that promotes healthy growth, especially of skin, hair, bones, and teeth.

____vitamin D____ 21. A vitamin known as the sunshine vitamin for strong bones and teeth.

____vitamin E____ 22. A vitamin found in fats and oils that protects cell membranes and aids in the use of energy foods.

____vitamin K____ 23. A vitamin that helps blood to clot properly.

____water____ 24. A nutrient that forms part of the blood, carries away waste products, and regulates body temperature.

____calories____ 25. Measure the amount of potential energy in food.

Food Diary

Name _____

Date _____ Period _____

Record all the foods, beverages, and snacks you eat in one day, then fill in the remainder of the chart. Using the Internet, log on to www.MyPyramid.com and select *MyPyramid Menu Planner*. Enter your age, gender, weight, height, and activity level to determine your recommended amounts from each of the food groups and record in the chart below. If you do not have access to a computer, refer to Figure 25-8 in the text. Select your calorie level to determine your recommended daily intakes. Finally, answer the questions below. **(Answers are student response.)**

Food	How Much?	Recommended Amounts from MyPyramid	Amount Over (+) or Under (-)
		Grains _____	_____
		Vegetables _____	_____
		Fruits _____	_____
		Milk _____	_____
		Meat and beans _____	_____
		Fats, oils, and sweets _____	_____

Review the amounts you were short or over in each food group. Then develop a list of changes you need to make in your eating patterns.

To improve my daily eating habits, I resolve to: **(Student response.)** _____

_____

_____

_____

_____

Are foods that supply certain nutrients missing from the list? **(Student response.)** _____

_____

_____

_____

Fast-Food Meals

Activity D

Name_____

Section 25:2

Date _____   Period _____

List your favorite fast-food meal in the space provided. Rate it for calories, fat, cholesterol, and sodium. Evaluate it for its contribution to your daily food plan by answering the questions that follow.
(Chart answers are student response.)

My Favorite Fast-Food Meal	Number of Calories	Grams of Fat	Cholesterol	Sodium

1. Identify foods in your meal from the grains group. **(Student response.)** _____

   _____

2. Identify foods in your meal from the vegetable group. **(Student response.)** _____

3. Identify foods in your meal from the fruit group. **(Student response.)** _____

4. Identify foods in your meal from the meat and beans group. **(Student response.)** _____

   _____

5. Identify foods in your meal from the milk group. **(Student response.)** _____

   _____

6. Identify foods in your meal that would be considered fats, oils, or sweets. **(Student response.)**

   _____

7. Are you missing foods from any of the groups listed above? If so, what changes could you make in your selections to improve the variety and balance of your meal? **(Student response.)**

   _____

8. Rate your meal based on its calorie, fat, cholesterol, and sodium content. Circle your responses. (*Poor* indicates that the content is too high, while *Excellent* indicates that the content is low.)

Calories:	Poor	Fair	Good	Excellent
Fat:	Poor	Fair	Good	Excellent
Cholesterol:	Poor	Fair	Good	Excellent
Sodium:	Poor	Fair	Good	Excellent

Comparing Food Prices

Name_____

Date _____ Period _____

Compare the prices of two different brands of food products and figure the unit price. Make sure you compare the same sizes. Then answer the question below. **(Chart answers are student response.)**

Food Item	Size/Quantity	Brand _____		Brand _____	
		Cost	Unit Price	Cost	Unit Price
1. Milk					
2. Cheese					
3. Yogurt					
4. Ketchup					
5. Canned tuna					
6. Macaroni					
7. Rice					
8. Corn tortillas					
9. Whole-wheat bread					
10. Canned corn					
11. Canned peaches					
12. Frozen peas					

What generalizations can you make about food prices and food brands? **(Student response.)** _____

_____

_____

_____

_____

Meeting Your Nutritional Needs

Activity F

Name _____

Section 25:4

Date _____ **Period** _____

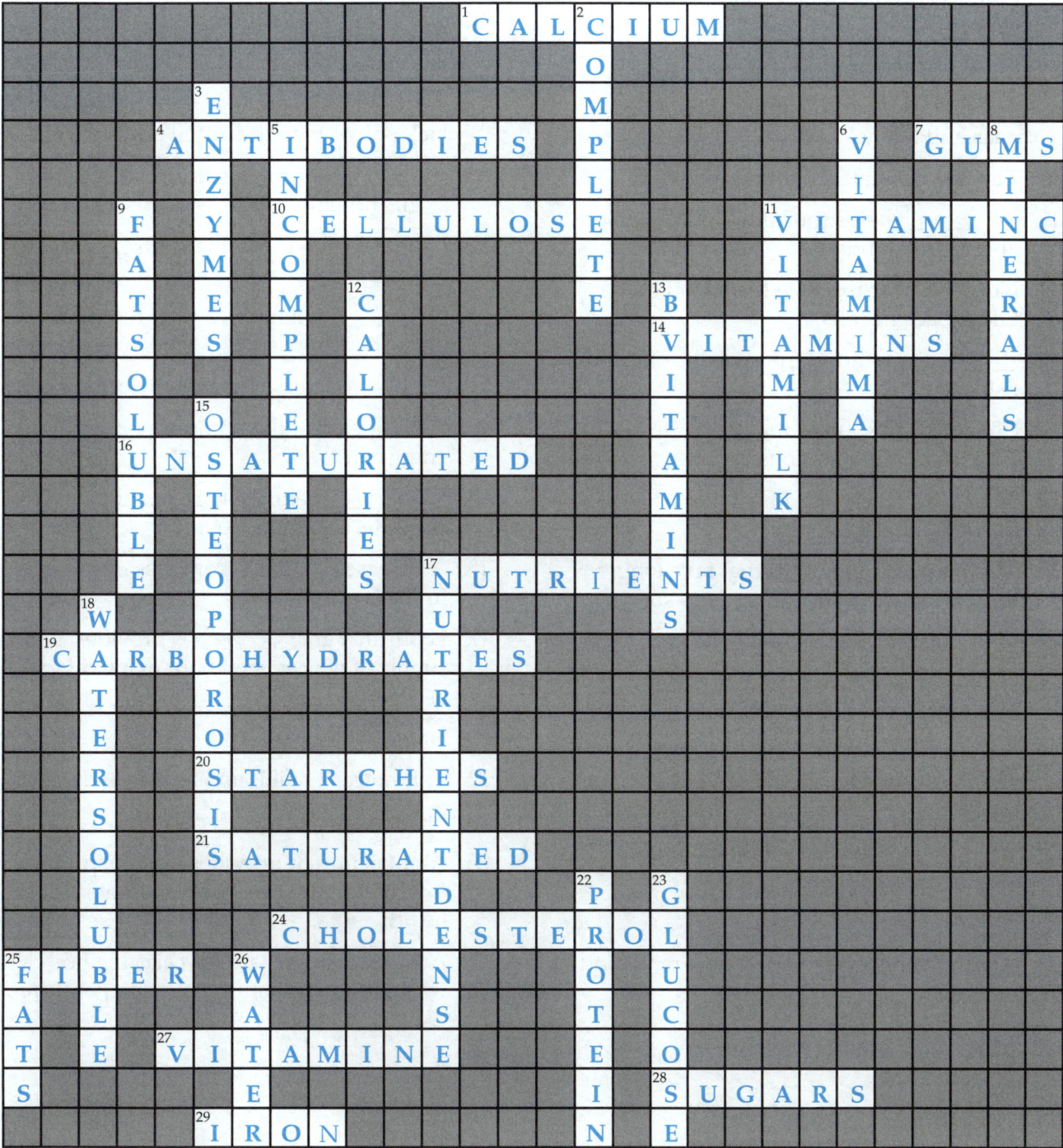

(Continued)

Chapter 25 Meeting Your Nutritional Needs

Read the descriptions and decide which chapter terms are being described. Write the correct terms in the crossword puzzle.

Across

1. A mineral found in milk and milk products needed for strong bones and teeth.
4. Proteins that fight off disease.
7. The dietary fiber in oatmeal and dried peas and beans.
10. The fibrous material found in plants.
11. _____ _____ helps the body fight infection and heal wounds.
14. Nutrients that regulate the action that takes place in cells.
16. _____ fats are found in vegetable oils and fish oils.
17. Chemical substances that the body needs to carry out its functions.
19. Sugars, starches, and fibers that provide a major source of energy.
20. Complex carbohydrates that take longer for the body to use as an energy source.
21. _____ fats increase the risk of heart disease.
24. A fat that helps the liver make bile, vitamin D, and sex hormones.
25. A form of carbohydrate that does not supply the body with energy but aids in digestion.
27. _____ _____ protects cell membranes and aids in the use of energy foods.
28. A quick source of energy.
29. A mineral needed to build new red blood cells.

Down

2. A _____ protein contains all the essential amino acids.
3. Proteins used to direct chemical reactions in the body.
5. _____ proteins are plant proteins and lack one or more essential amino acids.
6. _____ _____ promotes healthy bones, skin, and hair.
8. Nutrients needed to make strong bones and teeth.
9. _____-_____ vitamins are stored in the body in fatty tissue.
11. _____ _____ helps the blood clot properly.
12. _____ measure the amount of potential energy in food.
13. _____ _____ contribute to healthy nerves, appetite, and digestion.
15. A disease resulting from loss of calcium in the bones.
17. Foods that are _____ _____ provide a good supply of nutrients without many calories.
18. _____-_____ vitamins are lost in cooking water.
22. This nutrient builds and repairs body cells.
23. Blood sugar burned for energy.
25. A nutrient that provides energy, protects internal organs, and helps maintain healthy skin.
26. A nutrient important for carrying body wastes and regulating body temperature.

Chapter 26

Maintaining Your Health and Well-Being

Today's Health Problems

Activity A   Name _____

Section 26:1   Date _____   Period _____

For each disease listed below, describe the problem, identify its cause, and list its long-term effects. Then state how people can decrease their disease risk.

Disease	Description	Long-Term Effects	Steps to Decrease Risk
Arteriosclerosis	Fatty deposits called plaque form on the inner walls of the arteries. This cuts off the flow of blood to the heart and can result in a heart attack.	A heart attack occurs when a coronary artery becomes completely blocked.	Eat foods low in fat and cholesterol.
Hypertension	Blood pressure stays above the normal range. It causes the heart to work harder as it moves the blood through the circulatory system.	Increases the risk of stroke, which occurs when the pressure on the small vessels in the brain causes them to break. The blood supply to the brain is cut off and nerve cells cannot function.	Reduce excess weight, limit sodium (salt) in the diet, and take drugs that lower blood.
Cancer	Abnormal uncontrolled cell growth destroys healthy tissue.	Spread of cancer can result in destruction of organs and death.	Eat foods such as cabbage, broccoli, and cauliflower; foods high in vitamins A, C, and E; and insoluble fibers.

Follow the Guidelines

Activity B   Name _____

Section 26:1   Date _____ Period _____

Examine the following list of food items. Place a check (√) by food choices that fit well with the *Dietary Guidelines for Americans*. Place an *X* by food items that should be limited or reduced in the diet. Then answer the questions that follow.

__√__	Apples	__X__	French fries	__X__	Peanut butter
__X__	Bacon	__X__	Fried chicken	__√__	Popcorn
__√__	Baked fish	__X__	Hamburger	__√__	Raw cauliflower
__√__	Bananas	__X__	Hot dogs	__X__	Smoked sardines
__X__	Bologna	__X__	Hot fudge sundae	__√__	Soft-shell tacos
__√__	Brown rice	__√__	Lasagna	__X__	Steak
__√__	Celery	__√__	Lean chicken	__√__	Steamed broccoli
__X__	Chocolate cake	__√__	Mashed potatoes	__√__	Stir-fry vegetables
__X__	Doughnuts	__√__	Oatmeal-raisin cookie	__√__	Trimmed pork chops
__X__	Eggs	__√__	Orange juice	__√__	Whole-grain cereal
__√__	Fat-free milk	__√__	Pasta	__√__	Whole-wheat bread

1. Does what you eat make a difference in your health? Explain your answer. **Yes. Eating foods high in sodium or fat can result in health problems. Eating foods lower in fat and sodium and high in fiber can help prevent these problems.**

2. Why are fruits, vegetables, and whole-grain breads and cereals so important in the diet? **These foods contain fiber and other nutrients that help prevent health problems such as chronic disease.**

3. From the list above, name three examples of salt-cured, smoked, or nitrate-cured foods. **(List three:) bacon, hot dogs, smoked sardines**

A Healthy Weight Range

Activity C

Name _____

Section 26:2

Date _____ Period _____

Read the scenario below and follow individual directions in this three-part activity.

Anthony is a 25-year-old computer programmer who is at least 20 pounds overweight. He recalls his high school and college years when he was a star basketball player, fit and trim. Now, he realizes that several years at a desk job, fast-food lunches, and frequent snacks of potato chips and donuts has left him out of shape. He wants to get his weight under control.

Part One

Determine the following weight ranges for Anthony by checking Figure 26-5 in the text. (Anthony's height is 5 feet, 11 inches.)

1. Healthy weight range: ___133___ to ___177___ pounds

2. Overweight range: ___178___ to ___223___ pounds

3. Obese weight range: ___224___ pounds and above

Part Two

Anthony realizes that a large part of his problem is his poor diet. He rarely makes a meal since he lives alone. He prefers to grab a quick lunch on workdays and eat out with friends on weekends. In the space below, identify several ways that Anthony could improve his diet.

Recommended diet changes:

(Sample answer:) Anthony should start planning his meals. He should shop for ingredients for simple but nutritious meals he can make at home. He can make something to take for his lunch and cut back on eating out with his friends. When he does eat out, he should make healthful menu choices.

_____

_____

_____

_____

_____

_____

_____

_____

_____

_____

_____

_____

(Continued)

Part Three

Anthony's goal is to improve his diet and begin losing two pounds a week. He knows that he will need to burn 3,500 calories more than he takes in for each pound of weight loss, or a total of 7,000 calories per week. He plans to improve his diet, which would help him achieve his weight loss goal quicker. However, if he doesn't change his diet, he must become much more active. In the space below, identify several activities that Anthony could do to lose two pounds of body weight per week. (Use information from Figure 26-6 in the text.) **(Sample answers are given below.)**

Activity 1: **Walking (3 mph) 5** × _____30_____ = _____150_____
|Calorie expenditure per minute | Total minutes of activity | Total calories burned |

Activity 2: **Basketball 10** × _____25_____ = _____250_____
|Calorie expenditure per minute | Total minutes of activity | Total calories burned |

Activity 3: **Tennis (singles) 8** × _____60_____ = _____480_____
|Calorie expenditure per minute | Total minutes of activity | Total calories burned |

Activity 4: **Swimming 5** × _____60_____ = _____300_____
|Calorie expenditure per minute | Total minutes of activity | Total calories burned |

Activity 5: **Cycling (11 mph) 8** × _____60_____ = _____480_____
|Calorie expenditure per minute | Total minutes of activity | Total calories burned |

In the space below, summarize the weekly plan you propose for Anthony. State the activities he must perform and the required time he must spend doing each to lose two pounds each week. (The total calories burned by following your plan must equal 7,000.)
(Student response.)

_____
_____
_____
_____
_____
_____
_____
_____
_____
_____
_____
_____
_____

My Personal Fitness Plan

Activity D

Section 26:3

Name _____

Date _____ Period _____

Fill in the chart below with activities you could do as part of your personal fitness plan. In the first column, list activities you could do to help reach the recommended 60 minutes of moderate physical activity daily. Calculate the total number of minutes spent in a week on these activities and estimate the calories burned. **(Chart answers are sample responses. See Figure 26-6 in the text for calories.)**

Daily Activities	Average number of minutes per week	Number of calories burned each week:
Walk to school	15 min × 5 days = 75 min/week	3 cal/min=225 cal/week
Climb stairs between classes	2 min × 5 class breaks = 10 min × 5 days = 50 min/week	5 cal/ min= 250 cal/week
Shoot hoops after school with friends	30 min × 3 days = 90 min/week	5 cal/min = 450 cal/week
Help at home with household chores such as vacuuming, raking, mowing lawn	15 min x 6 days = 90 min/week	5 cal/min = 450 cal/week
Activities I can do for aerobic exercise:	**Average number of minutes per week:**	**Number of calories burned each week:**
Play basketball	60 min × 3 days = 180 min/week	10 cal/min = 1,800 cal/week
Activities I can do to strengthen muscles:	**Average number of minutes per week:**	**Number of calories burned each week:**
Lift weights	30 min × 2 days = 60 min/week	8 cal/min = 480 cal/week
Goal: Total 60 min/day, 420 min/week	**Total time for week:** 545 minutes	**Total calories burned:** 3,655

1. Consider the amount of physical activity identified and the calories burned. How long would it take to lose 5 pounds if you continued this workout plan and did not increase your intake of food? **(Student response.)**

    _____

2. What obstacles might prevent you from reaching a goal of 60 minutes of moderate activity each day? **(Student response.)**

    _____

    _____

Maintaining Your Health and Well-Being

Activity E

Section 26:4

Name _____

Date _____ Period _____

The completed crossword puzzle contains the following answers:

- 2 Across: ENDOMORPHS
- 6 Across: ANAEROBIC
- 7 Across: ECTOMORPHS
- 8 Across: DEPRESSANT
- 12 Across: WITHDRAWAL
- 14 Across: UNDERWEIGHT
- 15 Across: OVERWEIGHT
- 16 Across: FAD
- 18 Across: FLEXIBILITY
- 19 Across: DESIGNER
- 23 Across: TAR
- 24 Across: CARBONMONOXIDE
- 26 Across: BASALMETABOLISM
- 27 Across: IDEAL
- 28 Across: ARTERIOSCLEROSIS
- 30 Across: HALLUCINOGENS
- 31 Across: CALORIES
- 32 Across: AMPHETAMINES
- 33 Across: NARCOTICS
- 34 Across: CARCINOGENS

- 1 Down: SMOKE
- 3 Down: STIMULANT
- 4 Down: OBESITY
- 5 Down: EMPHYSEMA
- 9 Down: ECOND (SECONDHAND)
- 10 Down: SLEES
- 11 Down: STERK (STRESS)
- 13 Down: ANTIOXIDANTS
- 17 Down: ANOREXIA
- 20 Down: ALCOHOL
- 21 Down: HYDROGENATED
- 22 Down: HYPERTENSION
- 25 Down: LIVER
- 29 Down: AEROBIC

(Continued)

Read the descriptions and decide which chapter terms are being described. Write the correct terms in the crossword puzzle.

Across

2. People with a large frame and more rounded shape.

6. Exercises that use the muscles to produce a sudden burst of power as in doing push-ups.

7. People who have small bones and a slender, angular build.

8. A type of drug that slows the activity of the brain and knocks out control centers.

12. The condition of going without a substance to which the body is addicted.

14. A condition of weighing less than the ideal weight by 10 percent or more.

15. A condition of being up to 10 percent over ideal weight range.

16. _____ diets tend to be popular for a short period of time.

18. Stretching exercises increase _____.

19. Drugs that are chemically made to avoid present definitions of illegal drugs.

23. A brown, sticky mass found in the lungs of smokers.

24. When a person smokes, _____ _____ combines with the hemoglobin in the blood, leaving a person feeling lightheaded and short of breath.

26. The burning of calories to carry out the body's basic functions such as breathing and digestion. (two words)

27. Your _____ weight is a range within which your health is not affected by your weight.

28. Hardening of the arteries.

30. Psychedelic drugs that affect the mind.

31. _____ measure the amount of potential energy in food.

32. Pills that have been used to depress appetite, but prove ineffective in keeping off weight.

33. Drugs that depress the central nervous system and impair coordination.

34. Chemicals that cause cancer.

Down

1. _____ tobacco, such as chewing tobacco and snuff, are harmful to mouth tissues.

3. Drugs that speed up the central nervous system.

4. A condition of being at least 20 percent above ideal weight.

5. A disease in which the walls of the lungs are destroyed.

9. _____ smoke can be inhaled by a nonsmoker when someone is smoking nearby.

10. Occurs when the pressure on the small vessels in the brain causes them to break.

11. Muscle-building drugs with dangerous side effects.

13. _____, such as vitamins A, C, and E, prevent certain substances from harming body tissue.

17. _____ nervosa is self-starvation caused by an irrational fear of being overweight.

20. When ingested, this powerful depressant drug affects the brain and spinal cord.

21. A poisonous gas found in cigarette smoke. (two words)

22. A term for high blood pressure.

25. This organ produces enzymes that inactivate some cancer-causing carcinogens.

29. Exercise done at a moderate pace for a fairly long time using the large muscles.

Chapter 27

Managing Your Wardrobe

Clothing Speaks

Activity A

Name _____

Section 27:1

Date _____ **Period** _____

Clothing designs can enhance or play down certain body characteristics. Clip a picture of a garment from a magazine or catalog to illustrate each of the descriptions below. Then mount each one in the space provided. Under each example, explain how the garment you have chosen matches the description. **(Answers are student response.)**

1. **A garment that will make a person look taller.**

2. **A garment that will draw attention to a person's face.**

_____

_____

_____

_____

A Wardrobe Plan

Activity B

Section 27:1

Name_____

Date _____   Period _____

Evaluate your clothing needs by completing this wardrobe plan. List the activities you do and the basic garments you have for these activities. (Include colors, type, and style.) Then identify extenders and accessories that you need for each activity. Next, determine what items you need to buy. Prioritize this list, numbering the most important item *1*.   **(Answers are student response.)**

My Wardrobe Plan					
My Activities	**Basic Garments**	**Extenders**	**Accessories**	**Items I Need to Buy**	**Priority Number**

Be a Comparison Shopper

Activity C

Section 27:1

Name _____

Date _____ Period _____

Comparison shopping helps you gather information that you can use to get the best buy for your money. Choose one type of clothing item, such as jeans or a shirt. Then comparison shop for this item at four different stores. Read and record the information on the garment labels. Provide complete responses to the statements that follow. **(Answers are student response.)**

Store #1 _____

Article of Clothing _____

Label information:

Fabric content _____
_____
_____

Finishes _____
_____
_____

Care directions _____
_____
_____

Cost_____

Store #2 _____

Article of Clothing _____

Label information:

Fabric content _____
_____
_____

Finishes _____
_____
_____

Care directions _____
_____
_____

Cost _____

Store #3 _____

Article of Clothing _____

Label information:

Fabric content _____
_____
_____

Finishes _____
_____
_____

Care directions _____
_____
_____

Cost_____

Store #4 _____

Article of Clothing _____

Label information:

Fabric content _____
_____
_____

Finishes _____
_____
_____

Care directions _____
_____
_____

Cost_____

(Continued)

Name_____

1. Using the information you gathered, explain which clothing item you feel is the best buy. (Student response.)

_____

_____

_____

_____

_____

_____

_____

_____

_____

2. Explain how you would judge the quality of the clothing item. Look for smooth, flat, pucker-free seams, make sure the hem stitches do not show on the right side of the garment, and make sure the edge of the hem is finished. Also make sure buttons are securely attached and evenly spaced. Check that the zippers stay closed when the garment is stretched.

_____

_____

_____

_____

_____

3. Explain in detail how you would care for this item. (Student response.)

_____

_____

_____

_____

_____

_____

_____

_____

_____

How Clothing Performs

Read the following scenarios and respond to the questions that follow.

1. Beth purchased a wool jacket to wear on cool evenings with jeans. Check the following characteristics she can expect from this jacket.

   __✓__ A. Resists wrinkles.

   _____ B. Is washable.

   _____ C. Is cool and lightweight.

   __✓__ D. Weaker when wet.

   __✓__ E. Should be dry cleaned.

   _____ F. Builds up static electricity.

   __✓__ G. Can be eaten by moths.

   __✓__ H. Is durable and long lasting.

2. Pierre purchased a white silk shirt to wear for dressy special occasions. Check the following characteristics he can expect from this shirt.

   _____ A. Machine washes easily.

   _____ B. Is strong and durable.

   __✓__ C. Drapes in soft folds.

   _____ D. Responds well to bleach for removing perspiration stains.

   __✓__ E. Dry-cleans safely.

   __✓__ F. Resists wrinkles.

   _____ G. Does not absorb moisture.

   _____ H. Holds its shape well.

3. Erin purchased a pair of silver-colored pants that had a shiny finish. She was excited with the fashionable look of the pants and the label said *100% polyester*. How do you think these pants will wear?

   __✓__ A. Machine washes easily.

   _____ B. Breathes easily.

   _____ C. Stretches easily.

   __✓__ D. Stains easily.

   _____ E. Is comfortable to wear.

   __✓__ F. Is durable.

   __✓__ G. Fibers may break and pill.

   __✓__ H. Resists wrinkles.

4. Molly bought a dark-colored, two-piece outfit made of lightweight cotton fleece for her one-year-old nephew. The roomy pull-on pants and T- shirt displayed the emblem of the family's favorite football team. How do you think this outfit will wear?

   __✓__ A. Machine washes easily.

   _____ B. Should be dry-cleaned.

   __✓__ C. Is durable.

   _____ D. Builds up static electricity.

   __✓__ E. Is comfortable to wear.

   _____ F. May water spot.

   __✓__ G. Does not build up static.

   __✓__ H. May shrink if washed and dried at high temperatures.

Understanding Clothing Care Symbols

Activity E

Name _____

Section 27:2

Date _____ **Period** _____

Interpret the clothing care symbols and write the care instructions below each label.

90% NYLON

10% ELASTANE

EXCLUSIVE OF
DECORATION

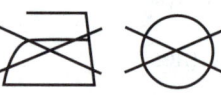

1. hand wash cold; only non-chlorine bleach; line dry; do not iron; do not dry clean

---

SHELL: 100% POLYESTER

LINING: 100% POLYESTER

FILLER: 70% DOWN CLUSTER
30% DOWN FEATHERS

REMOVE HOOD BEFORE
WASHING.

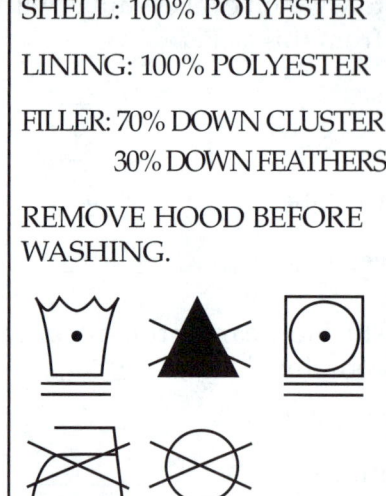

2. remove hood before washing; machine wash cold, gentle cycle; do not bleach; tumble dry low, gentle cycle; do not iron; do not dry clean

---

92% NYLON

8% SPANDEX

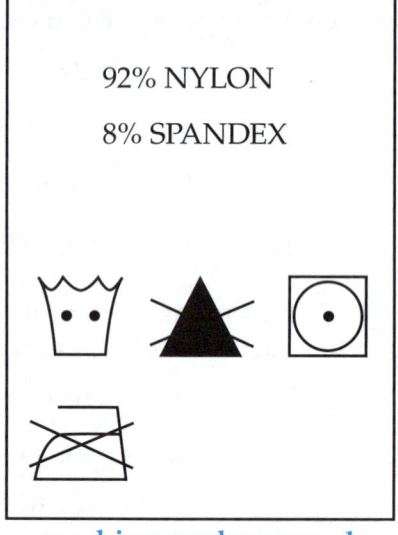

3. machine wash warm; do not bleach; tumble dry low; do not iron

---

100% WOOL

4. dry clean; do not wash; do not dry

100% ACRYLIC

5. machine wash cold, gentle cycle; only non-chlorine bleach; dry flat; low iron

---

60% COTTON

35% POLYESTER

5% SPANDEX

6. machine wash cold; only non-chlorine bleach; tumble dry low; medium iron

---

Chapter 28

Managing Your Housing

Housing Survey

Activity A   **Name** _____

Section 28:1   **Date** _____   **Period** _____

Complete the following survey. Then respond to the statement that follows.
(Answers are student response.)

1. I live in (type of home) _____

2. The people who live in my home include: _____

   _____

3. Check the statement that applies to you:

   _____ I have my own bedroom.   _____ I share a bedroom.

Often	Sometimes	Never	
_____	_____	_____	4. I eat meals at home.
_____	_____	_____	5. I eat meals away from home.
_____	_____	_____	6. I arrange the furniture in my room.
_____	_____	_____	7. I hang pictures on the walls of my room.
_____	_____	_____	8. I study in my room.
_____	_____	_____	9. I listen to music in my room.
_____	_____	_____	10. I keep my personal space neat and clean.
_____	_____	_____	11. I do hobbies in my room.

My hobbies include: _____

_____

12. When I am at home alone, my favorite place to spend time is _____

13. When I am at home with friends, my favorite place to spend time is _____

    Review your responses to the survey. In the space provided, list various physical, social, and emotional needs that your housing meets. These are considered the functions of your housing.
    (Student response.) _____

    _____

    _____

    _____

Types of Housing

Activity B

Name_____

Section 28:1

Date _____ Period _____

Describe each type of housing below. Then list the advantages and disadvantages of each.

Free-Standing House	
Description Separate home that is not connected to another unit.	
Advantages Privacy; Freedom; Considered an investment	**Disadvantages** More lawn care; Responsible for maintenance; Requires a large amount for a down payment; Must pay property taxes

Townhouse	
Description Homes that are built in rows or clusters with several units joined together.	
Advantages Have own entrance; Have own yard area; May own or rent in a more densely populated area, yet still have some privacy	**Disadvantages** Neighbors are very close; May be responsible for yard work

Duplexes	
Description Two units joined together.	
Advantages Still have own home, but usually at a lower cost than a free-standing home; Have freedom to make changes if duplex is owned; Have own entrance and yard	**Disadvantages** Close neighbors; Responsible for yard work

Apartments	
Description Common type of multifamily dwelling where several units are in one building.	
Advantages Usually rented, so amount of money needed to get into an apartment is less than buying a home; Can usually move at end of lease or with notice; May come furnished; may have utilities included	**Disadvantages** Have close neighbors; Space is usually limited; Less privacy; Noise restrictions; Less freedom to make changes to space

Condominiums	
Description Several units built together, but each unit is purchased as a separate home.	
Advantages Benefits of home ownership; Is an investment and should increase in value; Maintenance and insurance on the building is provided by the condo association; No extra yard work as condo association takes care of outdoor and shared areas	**Disadvantages** Have to pay a monthly fee to belong to the condo association; More expensive than renting as down payment is required; Noise restrictions may apply; Less privacy than a freestanding home

The Lease

Name _____

Date _____ Period _____

Examine the sample lease in Figure 28-4 in the text. Then answer the following questions.

1. This lease is a contract between ___two___ parties. Name them: Raoul and Ilse Doe, and Sawdusky Realty

2. To whom should Raoul and Ilse pay their rent? Lisa Brown

3. Whom should they contact if they develop a leaky sink? Mike Manning

4. Whom should they contact if they need to cancel their lease and move? Myra Lee

5. Raoul and Ilse may decide to move out at the end of their lease. If they do, how much notice are they required to give the landlord? 45 days before the end of the lease

6. Where do they pay rent? 1000 Collect St.

7. Can Raoul and Ilse sublet their apartment? no, unless they have prior written consent of the landlord

8. How much do they need for a security deposit? ___$950___ When will they get the security deposit back? 21 days after they vacate the premises

9. How long do the tenants have to notify the landlord of prior damages so they won't have to pay for existing repairs? seven days after beginning of lease

10. Under what conditions can the landlord enter the apartment to check the premises? at reasonable times and with 12 hours advance notice. Landlords may enter with less than 12 hours notice with tenant's permission or with no notice if a health or safety emergency exists.

11. Raoul and Ilse will be gone for one month in the summer. What could happen to their apartment and their belongings if they don't let the landlord know, in writing, that they will be gone? The landlord could assume abandonment after three weeks, rent to someone else, and sell all the tenant's property.

12. Can Raoul and Ilse keep a small dog in their apartment? no

What lease terms would concern you most if you were a tenant? Explain your answer. Student response.

_____

_____

What lease terms would concern you most if you were an apartment owner? Explain your answer. Student response.

_____

_____

Obtaining a Home

Activity D   Name_____

Section 28:1   Date _____ Period _____

Match the definitions related to buying, selling, or renting housing with the appropriate terms.

___B___ 1. An agreement between two or more parties; in real estate, usually written and legally binding.

___J___ 2. The person who leases an apartment from the property owner.

___C___ 3. The amount of money borrowed from a lending institution for the purchase of real estate.

___F___ 4. An amount of money a buyer must pay in order to borrow the rest from a lending institution.

___E___ 5. A spoken or written agreement between the renter and the property owner.

___G___ 6. A structure that houses more than one family.

___I___ 7. A sum of money put down to insure the landlord against the risk of loss due to unpaid rent or damages.

___D___ 8. This property owner has the right to determine the amount of rent and set rules and regulations for renters.

___H___ 9. A structure that houses one family.

___A___ 10. The purchasing and financing costs a buyer must pay at the time a loan is written or property sold.

A. closing costs
B. contract
C. down payment
D. landlord
E. lease
F. mortgage
G. multifamily dwelling
H. single-family dwelling
I security deposit
J. tenant

11. List three advantages of home ownership. **(List three:) emotional sense of security, freedom to do whatever you want to the home, money is invested in real estate, interest is deductible on federal income taxes**

12. List three disadvantages of home ownership. **(List three:) initial cost of down payment, cost of interest that is paid to the lending institution, cost of property taxes, time needed to sell home if you need to move, upkeep and repairs must be paid by owner**

13. What are three reasons for renting a home? **(List three:) don't need a large sum of money for down payment, don't have to pay property taxes, don't have to pay cost of maintenance, easier to move once terms of their contract are fulfilled, available in most areas**

Buying Furniture and Appliances

Activity E

Section 28:2

Name _____

Date _____   Period _____

Develop a buying plan for common home furnishings and appliances. Use the Internet to research a variety of stores, manufacturers, and prices. Comparison shop for three different types of each item and complete the chart below. **(Chart answers are student response.)**

Furnishing/ Appliance	Store	Price	Key Features
Sofa 1.			
2.			
3.			
Mattress 1.			
2.			
3.			
Refrigerator 1.			
2.			
3.			
Dishwasher 1.			
2.			
3.			
Dryer 1.			
2.			
3.			

Which items would you most likely purchase? Why? **(Student response.)** _____

_____

_____

Furniture in the Home

Activity F   **Name** _____

Section 28:2   **Date** _____   **Period** _____

Find a picture of a furnished room you like and mount it in the space below. Then answer the questions about the furniture choices in the room.

1. Do any of the furniture pieces serve more than one function? (Student response.) _____

   _____

   _____

2. Does the furniture appear to fit the space well? What other furniture would you add to the room? Is there any furniture you would take out of the room? (Student response.) _____

   _____

   _____

3. Describe the room's appearance of comfort or lack of it. (Student response.) _____

   _____

   _____

4. Which furniture pieces appear portable or easily moved? Which do not? (Student response.) ____

   _____

   _____

   _____

5. How could you identify whether the pieces of furniture were good quality? (Student response.)

   _____

   _____

6. What specific care requirements might this furniture need? (Student response.) _____

   _____

   _____

Chapter 29

Managing Your Transportation

Choosing a Mode of Transportation

Activity A   **Name**_____

Section 29:1   **Date** _____ **Period** _____

Use the decision-making process to consider two different modes of transportation. (Review the decision-making process outlined in Chapter 4 of the text.) Then determine which transportation choice would best meet your needs and resources by answering the following questions.

1. What are your transportation needs? (Student response.)_____
   _____
   _____
   _____
   _____

2. What are your options? In what ways can you meet your transportation needs? (Student response.)
   _____
   _____
   _____
   _____

3. For each option, what information do you have? (Consider the pro and con of each option as well as your personal feelings.) (Student response.)_____
   _____
   _____
   _____
   _____
   _____
   _____
   _____
   _____
   _____

(Continued)

4. Which option seems best for you? Why? (Student response.)

_____

_____

_____

_____

_____

_____

_____

_____

_____

5. What steps do you need to take to follow through with this option? (Develop a plan of action.)
(Student response.)

_____

_____

_____

_____

_____

_____

_____

_____

6. Evaluate your final plan. Are there any important factors that you did not consider earlier?
(Student response.)

_____

_____

_____

_____

_____

_____

_____

_____

Choosing a Car

Activity B   Name _____

Section 29:2   Date _____ Period _____

Search the Internet and find a car for sale that interests you, or visit a car lot and gather similar information. Complete the following using the information you locate. **(Chart answers are student response.)**

Questions	Information Gathered
1. What is the make and model of the car that interests you?	
2. What features are offered on this particular vehicle?	
3. What is the odometer reading on this vehicle?	
4. What is the sticker price (or asking price) for this vehicle?	
5. What is the listed retail price for this vehicle in the *NADA Official Used Car Guide*? (Consider features and the odometer reading.)	
6. Which features added to the base cost of the vehicle?	
7. What amounts, if any, did you have to subtract from the current retail price for this car? (Example: high mileage)	
8. What is the estimated loan value on this car?	
9. What is the estimated miles per gallon (MPG) for this vehicle?	
10. What kind of warranty is offered with this vehicle?	
11. How does the seller's asking price compare to the average retail price you calculated using the NADA guide?	
12. Calculate the cost of purchasing this car if you paid the asking price to the seller, paid the sales tax in your area, purchased license plates, and registered the title in your name.	Asking price: Sales tax: License Plates: Title and Registration Fees: Total Cost of Purchase:
13. Contact an insurance agent in your area and ask for a quote for this vehicle for a teenage driver with at least 50/100/50 for liability coverage.	